STAND OUT

Evidence-Based Learning for College and Career Readiness

2

THIRD EDITION

WORKBOOK

ROB JENKINS

STACI JOHNSON

NATIONAL GEOGRAPHIC LEARNING | CENGAGE Learning

Australia • Brazil • Mexico • Singapore • United Kingdom • United States

Stand Out 2: Evidence-Based Learning for College and Career Readiness, Third Edition
Rob Jenkins and Staci Johnson
Workbook

Publisher: Sherrise Roehr
Executive Editor: Sarah Kenney
Development Editor: Lewis Thompson
Assistant Editor: Patricia Giunta
Director of Global Marketing: Ian Martin
Executive Marketing Manager: Ben Rivera
Product Marketing Manager: Dalia Bravo
Media Researcher: Leila Hishmeh
Director of Content and Media Production: Michael Burggren
Production Manager: Daisy Sosa
Senior Print Buyer: Mary Beth Hennebury
Cover and Interior Designer: Brenda Carmichael
Composition: Lumina
Cover Image: Portra Images/Getty Images
Bottom Images: (Left to Right) Jay B Sauceda/Getty Images; Tripod/Getty Images; Portra Images/Getty Images; Portra Images/Getty Images; Dear Blue/Getty Images; Hero Images/Getty Images; Jade/Getty Images; Seth Joel/Getty Images; LWA/Larry Williams/Getty Images; Dimitri Otis/Getty Images

Work Book
ISBN 13: 978-1-305-65549-2

National Geographic Learning/Cengage Learning
20 Channel Center Street
Boston, MA 02210
USA

Cengage Learning is a leading provider of customized learning solutions with office locations around the globe, including Singapore, the United Kingdom, Australia, Mexico, Brazil and Japan. Locate our local office at: **international.cengage.com/region**

Visit National Geographic Learning online at **NGL.Cengage.com**
Visit our corporate website at **www.cengage.com**

Printed in the United States of America
Print Number: 12 Print Year: 2023

CONTENTS

TO THE TEACHER

ABOUT THE SERIES

The **Stand Out** series is designed to facilitate *active* learning within life-skill settings that lead students to career and academic pathways. Each student book and its supplemental components in the six-level series expose students to competency areas most useful and essential for newcomers with careful treatment of level appropriate but challenging materials. Students grow academically by developing essential literacy and critical thinking skills that will help them find personal success in a changing and dynamic world.

STAND OUT WORKBOOK

The **Stand Out Workbook** is designed to provide additional practice for learners to reinforce what they learned in each student book lesson. It can be used as homework or a supplement to the lesson in the classroom. Each lesson in **Stand Out** is driven by a life-skill objective and supported by vocabulary and grammar. Students are not expected to master or acquire vocabulary and grammar completely after being exposed to it just one time, hence the need for additional practice. The lessons in the student book are three pages long and each supporting workbook lesson is also three pages long. The workbook lessons correlate directly with the student book lessons.

The **Stand Out Workbook** establishes a link to new content by providing the essential vocabulary introduced in the books often in a way that also promotes critical thinking skills. Promoting critical thinking skills is essential for students to become independent lifelong learners. About half of the three-page practice is grammar focused where students are given a chart with notes, study how the grammar facilitates communication, and gain additional needed confidence through practice.

HOW TO USE THE STAND OUT WORKBOOK

The workbook can be used in the following ways:

1. The activities in the workbook can be used as additional practice during the class to reinforce one or more practice activities in the student book.
2. The activities in the workbook can be assigned as homework. This is often a good way to reinforce what students have learned. The skills, vocabulary, and structures may not transfer into long-term memory after the lesson, so reinforcing the lesson after a short period of time away can be very helpful. Additionally, teachers can also review the homework at the beginning of each class, giving students another opportunity to be exposed to the information. Reviewing the homework is also a good strategy for the *Warm-up/Review* portion of the lesson and can be used in place of the one proposed in the **Stand Out Lesson Planner**.
3. The **Stand Out Workbook** can be used as a tool in the flipped classroom. In flipped classrooms, students prepare for lessons away from class before they are presented. Since the **Stand Out Workbook** introduces much of the vocabulary and grammar for each lesson, it is ideal for incorporating this approach.

ADDITIONAL PRACTICE

The **Stand Out** series is a comprehensive one-stop for all student needs. There is no need to look any further than the resources offered. Additional practice is available through the online workbook, which is different from the print workbook. There are also hundreds of multi-level worksheets available online. Please visit ngl.cengage.com/so3 to get easy access to all resources.

LESSON 1 Nice to meet you!

GOAL ■ Greet people and describe feelings

A. Read and practice the conversations.

Jackie: Hello, Veronica. How are you?
Veronica: Hi, Jackie. I'm angry.
Jackie: Why?
Veronica: My brother is lying to me.

Frank: Hello, Jennifer. How are you?
Jennifer: Hi, Frank. I'm happy.
Frank: Why?
Jennifer: It's my birthday!

Mario: Hello, Chau. How are you?
Chau: Hello, Mario. I'm sad.
Mario: Why?
Chau: I have a headache.

Hector: Hello, Cecil. How are you?
Cecil: Hi, Hector. I'm happy.
Hector: Me, too.
Cecil: It's a great day!

B. Answer questions about the conversations in Exercise A.

1. Who is happy? ____________________
2. Who is angry? ____________________
3. Why is she angry? ____________________
4. Who is sad? ____________________
5. Why is he sad? ____________________

C. Look at the information and read the conversation.

Name: Mario
Feeling: fine

Name: Katrina
Feeling: tired

Name: Alexi
Feeling: hungry

Name: Lien
Feeling: angry

Mario: Hi, Katrina. How are you?
Katrina: Hello, Mario. I'm tired. I need some rest. How are you?
Mario: I'm fine. Thanks.

D. Write conversations using the information from Exercise C.

Alexi: ____

Lien: ____

Alexi: ____

Mario: ____

Lien: ____

Mario: ____

Alexi: ____

Katrina: ____

Alexi: ____

Alexi: ____

Mario: ____

Alexi: ____

E. Read the chart.

<table>
<tr><th colspan="4">Simple Present: Be (Contractions)</th></tr>
<tr><th>Subject</th><th>Be</th><th>Feeling</th><th>Example sentence</th></tr>
<tr><td>I</td><td>am</td><td rowspan="3">fine
nervous
sad
tired
happy
angry
hungry</td><td>I am fine. (I'm fine.)</td></tr>
<tr><td>You, We, They</td><td>are</td><td>You are tired. (You're tired.)
We are hungry. (We're hungry.)
They are nervous. (They're nervous.)</td></tr>
<tr><td>He, She, It</td><td>is</td><td>He is happy. (He's happy.)
She is angry. (She's angry.)</td></tr>
</table>

F. Complete the sentences with the correct form of *be*. Then, write the contractions.

1. I ___am___ tired. I need some rest. — 1. ___I'm___ tired.
2. Maria and Paul ________ hungry. — 2. ________ hungry.
3. We ________ fine. How are you? — 3. ________ fine.
4. He ________ angry. He needs our help. — 4. ________ angry.
5. The children ________ nervous. It's exam day. — 5. ________ nervous.
6. She ________ happy. She has good friends. — 6. ________ happy.
7. You ________ sad. Can I help you? — 7. ________ sad.
8. The dog ________ hungry. Feed it, please. — 8. ________ hungry.

G. Match the sentences with the feelings. Draw lines.

1. She needs some rest.	a. sad
2. They have a test today.	b. hungry
3. We have a new baby!	c. nervous
4. He wants a hamburger.	d. tired
5. I have no friends.	e. happy

H. Write sentences with the information from Exercise G.

1. She's tired. She needs some rest.
2. ________________________________
3. ________________________________
4. ________________________________
5. ________________________________

LESSON 2 What's your name and number?

GOAL Complete a registration form

A. Read the registration form and answer the questions.

Sherman Adult School Registration Form

PERSONAL INFORMATION

Name:	Nguyen (Last) Lien (First)	**Date:**	01/25
Date of Birth:	07/02/1987	**Phone:**	(909) 555-6387
Street Address:	99 Jackson Street		
City:	Riverside	**State:** CA	**Zip Code:** 92503

1. When did Lien complete the form? ______________________
2. What is Lien's last name? ______________________
3. What is Lien's date of birth? ______________________
4. What's the name of the school? ______________________
5. What's Lien's area code? ______________________
6. Where does Lien live? ______________________

B. Read the registration form.

Evans Adult School Registration Form

PERSONAL INFORMATION

Name: ____________ ____________ **Date:** ____________
Last First

Date of Birth: ____________ **Phone:** (   ) ____________

Street Address: ____________

City: ____________ **State:** ____________ **Zip Code:** ____________

C. Write the information in the form in Exercise B.

Jonathan Smith	(714)	January 14th
555-8989	March 3rd, 1978	Pine City
California	2356 Orchard Lane	90638

D. Read the chart.

Possessive Adjectives		
Pronoun	**Possessive adjective**	**Example sentence**
I	**My**	**My** address is 3356 Archer Blvd.
You	**Your**	**Your** phone number is 555-5678.
He	**His**	**His** last name is Jones.
She	**Her**	**Her** first name is Lien.
It	**Its**	**Its** name is Crystal River Dam.
We	**Our**	**Our** teacher is Mr. Kelley.
They	**Their**	**Their** home is in Sausalito.

E. Complete the sentences with possessive adjectives.

1. I live in a big house. ____My____ house is on Orchard Lane.
2. Please call Maria and Jonathan. ____________ phone number is 555-8989.
3. You have a new zip code. ____________ zip code is 90638.
4. We need a delivery, please. ____________ address is 2356 Orchard Lane.
5. He lives in a big city. ____________ city is next to Riverton.
6. Maria's husband is young. ____________ date of birth is March 3rd, 1978.
7. The motel is famous. ____________ name is Dew Drop Inn.

F. Complete the sentences using the information below.

Name: Kenji Nakamura

School: Lincoln Adult School

Home Address: 2274 W. Bayside Drive, San Francisco, CA

Date of Birth: August 12th, 1985

Name: Marie Alexander

School: Lincoln Adult School

Home Address: 32 W. Palm Drive, San Francisco, CA

Date of Birth: June 5th, 1975

1. Kenji lives in an apartment. ____________ address is ________________________.
2. Marie and Kenji go to school. ____________ school is ________________________.
3. Marie is older than Kenji. ____________ date of birth is ________________________.
4. Marie and Kenji live in the same state. ____________ state is ________________________.
5. Kenji is from Japan. ____________ last name is ________________________.

PRE-UNIT

LESSON 3 Open your books!

GOAL ■ Follow instructions

A. Look at the picture and complete the sentences with information from the box.

is reading	are doing	is listening
is talking	is writing	is standing

1. Edgar ______________________________ on a piece of paper.
2. Julie ______________________________ a book.
3. Shiro ______________________________ to a recording.
4. Sara ______________________________ to a student.
5. Shiro, Julie, and Edgar ______________________________ class assignments.
6. Sara ______________________________ near her desk.

B. Read the paragraph.

A teacher needs to talk to many students at the same time. It is important that students participate. They need the practice. Ask for help when you don't understand. Speak in English for practice. Talk to the teacher, and he or she will help you. You can say, "I don't understand." You can also ask the teacher or your classmates questions. For example, one question could be, "Can you say that again?"

C. Read the sentences and questions.

Please speak slower.	I'm sorry. I don't understand.	Excuse me?
Please speak louder.	Can you say that again, please?	Can you spell that?

D. Which sentences and questions do you say more? Rank them in order of how often you use them. *1* is the most often and *6* is the least often used.

__________ I'm sorry. I don't understand.

__________ Please speak slower.

__________ Please speak louder.

__________ Excuse me?

__________ Can you say that again, please?

__________ Can you spell that?

E. Read the chart.

Questions with *Can*			
Question word	Subject	Verb	Example sentence
can	you	help answer repeat say speak spell	**Can** you help me? **Can** you answer the question? **Can** you repeat it, please? **Can** you say it again, please? **Can** you speak slower? **Can** you spell that, please?

F. Use the words to write questions.

1. you / spell that / can — *Can you spell that?*
2. say that again / can / you ______
3. that / you / can / repeat ______
4. speak louder / you / can ______
5. can / you / help me ______
6. you / slower / can / speak ______
7. English / you / teach me / can ______
8. open the door / can / you ______
9. write it / you / can ______

G. Match the problems with the questions.

1. The teacher speaks very fast.	a. Can I talk to you after class?
2. The room is hot.	b. Can you repeat that?
3. You didn't hear it all.	c. Can you speak slower?
4. You don't know how to write it.	d. Can you spell that, please?
5. You need to talk to the teacher.	e. Can you turn on the air-conditioning?

H. Read the conversation and write a new one. Use ideas from Exercise G.

Student A: I have a problem. Can you help me?

Student B: Sure.

Student A: You speak very fast. Can you speak slower?

Student B: OK.

Student A: ______

Student B: ______

Student A: ______

Student B: ______

UNIT 1

LESSON 1 Where are you from?

GOAL ■ Ask for and give personal information

A. Read about the students and complete the table.

Kenji	Anya	Gilberto	Marie
single 22 years old Los Angeles	married 68 years old Los Angeles	single 30 years old Los Angeles	divorced 32 years old Los Angeles

Name	Marital status	Age	Residence
Kenji	*single*		
Anya			
Gilberto			
Marie			

B. Look at the information and complete the registration form.

Alex Stoddard 22 Long Island Lane New York City New York	08601 November 21st, 1970 Married (646) 555-3465

Pleasanton Adult School Registration Form

Name: ______________ ______________ **Phone:** ( )
Last First

Marital Status: ______________ **Date of Birth:** ______________

Residence: ______________________________

____

C. Read the paragraph and answer the questions. Study paragraph formatting.

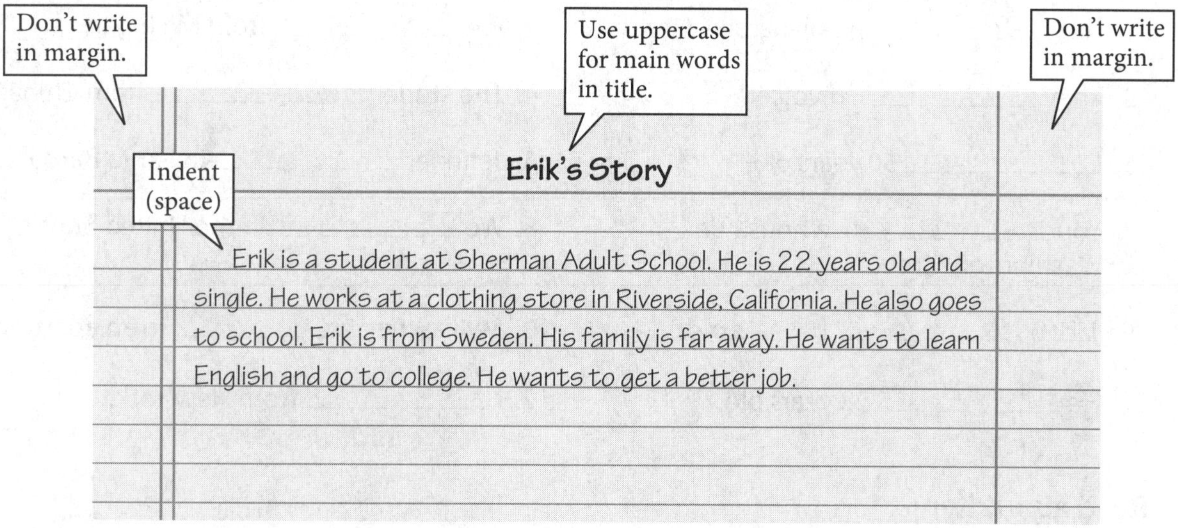

1. Where is Erik from? ______________________
2. Where does he live? ______________________
3. What is his marital status? ______________________
4. What is his age? ______________________

D. Read the charts.

Simple Present: *Live*			
Subject	**Verb**	**Residence**	**Example sentence**
I, We, You, They	live	in Los Angeles in California in the United States in Mexico	I **live** in Los Angeles. You **live** in Los Angeles, California.
He, She	lives		He **lives** in the United States. She **lives** in Mexico.

Simple Present: *Be*			
Subject	**Verb**	**Information**	**Example sentence**
I	am	from Mexico single 23 years old divorced from Vietnam	I **am** *(I'm)* from Mexico.
We, You, They	are		We **are** *(We're)* single. You **are** *(You're)* 23 years old.
He, She	is		He **is** *(He's)* divorced. She **is** *(She's)* from Vietnam.

E. Complete the sentences with the correct form of *live* or *be*.

1. He ___lives___ in Tallahassee, Florida.
2. We __________ from Michigan.
3. They __________ divorced.
4. The students __________ from China.
5. I __________ 50 years old.
6. Jennifer __________ in Santa Barbara.
7. You __________ in a house on Washington Street.
8. We __________ in the United States.
9. Jacob __________ 18 years old.
10. My teacher __________ in an apartment.
11. He __________ 28 years old.
12. I __________ from New York.

F. Read about Kenji.

This is Kenji. He is from Japan. Kenji is a student. He lives in Los Angeles. He is 22 years old. He is single.

G. Write paragraphs about Anya and Gilberto from Exercise A.

This is Anya. ____

____

____

____

This is Gilberto. ____

____

____

____

H. Write a paragraph about yourself on a separate piece of paper. Include your name, age, marital status, where you are from, and where you live. Use correct paragraph formatting.

UNIT 1

LESSON 2 Kenji's family

GOAL ■ Identify family relationships

A. Complete as much as you can about yourself.

GRANDPARENTS: Father's Side

____
Grandfather

____
Grandmother

____

____
Children

GRANDPARENTS: Mother's Side

____
Grandfather

____
Grandmother

____

____
Children

PARENTS

____
Father

____
Mother

____

____
Children

Me

____
My name

____
My spouse

____

____
My children

B. Read about Lien and answer the questions.

My name is Lien Nguyen. I have a wonderful family. I have three sisters and one brother. We live with our mother and father in the United States. I also have aunts and an uncle here. One of my sisters still lives in Vietnam. My mother has three sisters. She doesn't have a brother. My father has one brother and one sister.

1. How many sisters does Lien have? ______________________________
2. How many uncles does Lien have? ______________________________
3. How many aunts does Lien have? ______________________________
4. Where is Lien from? ______________________________
5. Where do Lien's mother and father live? ______________________________
6. What's Lien's last name? ______________________________

C. Read the charts.

Simple Present: *Have*

Subject	*Have*	Information	Example sentence
I, You, We, They	have	three brothers two sisters	I **have** three brothers. We **have** two sisters.
He, She	has	no cousins three sons	He **has** no cousins. She **has** three sons.

Simple Present Negative: *Have*

Subject	Negative	*Have*	Information	Example sentence
I, You, We, They	don't	have	three brothers two sisters	I **don't have** three brothers. We **don't have** two sisters.
He, She	doesn't		cousins three sons	He **doesn't have** cousins. She **doesn't have** three sons.

D. Circle the correct sentence.

1. I have two sisters. / I has two sisters.
2. I doesn't have a wife. / I don't have a wife.
3. You don't have an aunt in Korea. / You doesn't have an aunt in Korea.
4. Ken have a brother. / Ken doesn't have a brother.
5. My mother have four sisters. / My mother has four sisters.
6. You doesn't have a niece in Poland. / You don't have a niece in Poland.
7. Maria doesn't have a husband. / Maria don't have a husband.
8. We doesn't have children. / We don't have children.
9. Jessica and Kate has a brother. / Jessica and Kate have a brother.

E. Look at the diagram.

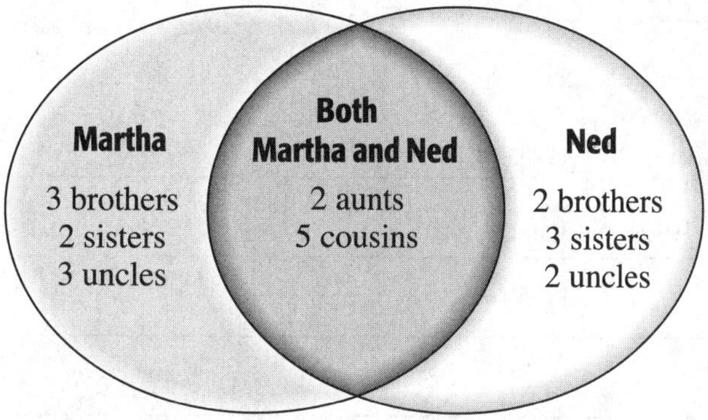

F. Write sentences using the information in Exercise E.

1. Martha has three brothers.
2. ______
3. ______
4. ______
5. ______
6. ______

G. Write sentences about your family.

EXAMPLE: I have three brothers and two sisters.

1. ______
2. ______
3. ______
4. ______

UNIT 1

LESSON 3 Kenji's class

GOAL ■ Describe people

A. Study the charts and write sentences.

Pronoun	*Have*
I, You, We, They	have
He, She, It	has

Pronoun	*Be*
I	am
You, We, They	are
He, She, It	is

Name	Hair *have/has*	Eyes *have/has*	Height *am/is/are*	Weight *am/is/are*
Neda	brown	brown	5′6″	140
Saul	black	brown	5′8″	185
Pamela	blond	blue	5′5″	120
Connie	red	green	5′5″	125
			(5′6″ ***tall***)	(140 ***pounds***)

1. Neda is 5'6" tall and 140 pounds.
2. Saul and Neda have ______________________.
3. Pamela is ______________________.
4. Pamela has ______________________.
5. Connie and Pamela are ______________________.
6. Neda has ______________________.

B. Write sentences about yourself.

Hair: ______________________

Eyes: ______________________

Height: ______________________

Weight: ______________________

C. Read about the three men.

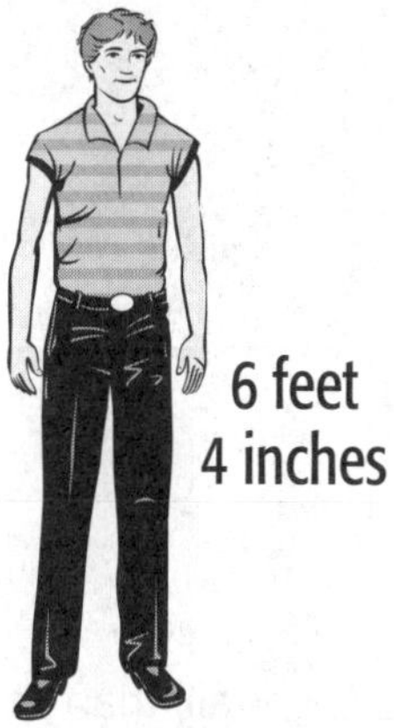

Howard
green eyes
blond hair
tall

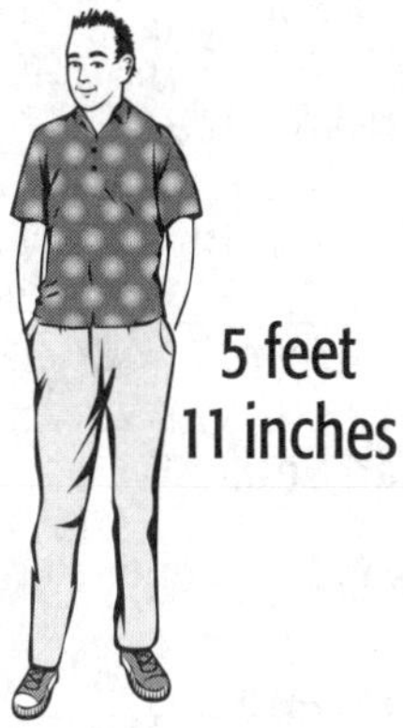

Sam
brown eyes
brown hair
average height

Kyle
blue eyes
brown hair
short

D. Write about the men in Exercise C.

Howard 1. *Howard is tall.*

2. *He has blond hair and green eyes.*

Sam 3. ____________________

4. ____________________

Kyle 5. ____________________

6. ____________________

E. Read the chart.

Comparative and Superlative Adjectives		
Adjective	Comparative adjectives	Superlative adjectives
tall	taller (Steve is **taller <u>than</u>** Dalva.)	**tallest**
short	shorter (Dalva is **shorter <u>than</u>** Kenji.)	**shortest**
heavy	heavier (Gilberto is **heavier <u>than</u>** Lien.)	**heaviest**
thin	thinner (Marie is **thinner <u>than</u>** Sung.)	**thinnest**
old	older (Anya is **older <u>than</u>** Ahmed.)	**oldest**
young	younger (Mario is **younger <u>than</u>** Steve.)	**youngest**

F. Complete the sentences with comparative adjectives.

1. John is ______taller______ (tall) than Oscar.
2. Cynthia is ____________ (short) than Oscar.
3. Herbert is ____________ (heavy) than Huyen.
4. Lien is ____________ (thin) than Huyen.
5. Jack is ____________ (young) than Leti.
6. Frank is ____________ (old) than Leti.
7. Kim is ____________ (thin) than Jim and ____________ (tall) than Karen.
8. Maria is ____________ (tall) and ____________ (thin) than Kim.

G. Answer the questions about Exercise F.

1. Who is the tallest—Oscar, Cynthia, or John? ____________
2. Who is heavier—Herbert or Huyen? ____________
3. Who is heavier—Herbert or Lien? ____________
4. Who is the thinnest—Herbert, Lien, or Huyen? ____________
5. Who is the youngest—Jack, Leti, or Frank? ____________
6. Who is the oldest—Jack, Leti, or Frank? ____________
7. Who is the thinnest—Kim, Jim, or Maria? ____________

H. Look at the information and write sentences with comparative and superlative adjectives.

So

Duong

Tan

1. ____________
2. ____________
3. ____________
4. ____________

UNIT 1

LESSON 4 My schedule

GOAL ■ Interpret and write schedules

A. Read the paragraph about Lidia's schedule and complete the planner page for her.

Lidia is married and has three children. She is a student at the local adult school. Every morning, she wakes up at 6:00 a.m. She helps her children get ready, and she takes them to school at 8:00 a.m. One hour later at nine o'clock, she goes to school. At three in the afternoon, Lidia's children come home, and she helps them with homework until her husband comes home at 5:30 p.m. The family usually eats dinner at 6:30 p.m. At eight o'clock in the evening, Lidia and her husband put the kids to bed. Then, they watch TV or read until they go to bed at 10:00 p.m.

9:44 AM

September 29th Day | Week | Month | Tasks 29

MORNING		AFTERNOON		EVENING	
5:00 a.m.		12:00 p.m.		6:00 p.m.	
5:30		12:30	eat lunch	6:30	
6:00		1:00		7:00	
6:30		1:30	take a 15-minute break	7:30	
7:00		2:00		8:00	
7:30		2:30		8:30	
8:00		3:00		9:00	
8:30		3:30		9:30	
9:00		4:00		10:00	
9:30		4:30		10:30	
10:00		5:00			
10:30		5:30			
11:00					
11:30					

B. Read Kim's calendar.

Monday	Tuesday	Wednesday	Thursday
15 7:00 a.m. go to school 9:00 a.m. take a break 12:30 p.m. go to work	**16** 7:00 a.m. watch kids 10:00 a.m. go to the store 12:30 p.m. go to work	**17** 7:00 a.m. go to school 9:00 a.m. take a break 12:30 p.m. go to work	**18** 7:00 a.m. watch kids 9:00 a.m. study 12:30 p.m. go to work
22 7:00 a.m. go to school 9:00 a.m. take a break 12:30 p.m. go to work	**23** 7:00 a.m. watch kids 10:00 a.m. go to the store 12:30 p.m. go to work	**24** 7:00 a.m. go to school 9:00 a.m. take a break 12:30 p.m. go to work	**25** 7:00 a.m. watch kids 9:00 a.m. study 12:30 p.m. go to work

C. Circle the correct answers about the calendar in Exercise B.

1. What does Kim do Monday through Thursday?
   a. She goes to school.
   b. She goes to the store.
   c. She goes to work.

2. When does Kim watch the kids?
   a. She watches the kids on Tuesday and Thursday in the morning.
   b. She watches the kids on Tuesday and Thursday in the evening.
   c. She watches the kids every day.

3. How often does Kim go to the store?
   a. She goes to the store once a week.
   b. She goes to the store twice a week.
   c. She goes to the store every morning.

D. Read the chart.

Simple Present			
Subject	**Verb**	**Information**	**Example sentence**
I, You, We, They	eat go help play	lunch to school with the children soccer	I always **eat** lunch at 4:00 p.m. You often **go** to school at 8:00 a.m. We sometimes **help** with the children. They never **play** soccer on Saturday.
He, She	eats goes helps plays	lunch to school with the children soccer	He rarely **eats** lunch at 12:00 p.m. Nadia always **goes** to school early. Gilberto never **helps** with the children. She sometimes **plays** soccer on Friday.

E. Rewrite each sentence with the new subject in parentheses.

1. I wake up at 6:00 a.m. (Anya) Anya wakes up at 6:00 a.m.
2. Ivan gets up at 7:00 a.m. (you) ____________________
3. We go to work at 8:00 a.m. (Ivan) ____________________
4. Anya helps with the grandchildren. (they) ____________________
5. Vladimir and Ziven play soccer. (we) ____________________
6. You work in Los Angeles. (Ivan) ____________________
7. The children go to school. (I) ____________________
8. I take the children to the beach. (Anya) ____________________

F. Complete each sentence with the verb and frequency word in parentheses.

1. (wake up / often) Gilberto often wakes up at 5:00 a.m.
2. (work / always) He ____________________ at his father's restaurant.
3. (take / sometimes) His children ____________________ the bus to school.
4. (play / often) His friends ____________________ soccer on Sunday.
5. (work / sometimes) On Mondays, she ____________________ overtime.
6. (get up / rarely) I ____________________ at 6:00 a.m.
7. (wake up / sometimes) My brother ____________________ at 7:00 a.m.
8. (take / rarely) We ____________________ the bus to work.

G. Write sentences about Lidia in Exercise A.

1. Lidia wakes up every day at 6:00 a.m.
2. ____________________
3. ____________________
4. ____________________
5. ____________________
6. ____________________

UNIT 1

LESSON 5 How is the weather today?

GOAL ■ Interpret information about weather

A. Look at the weather forecast and write sentences.

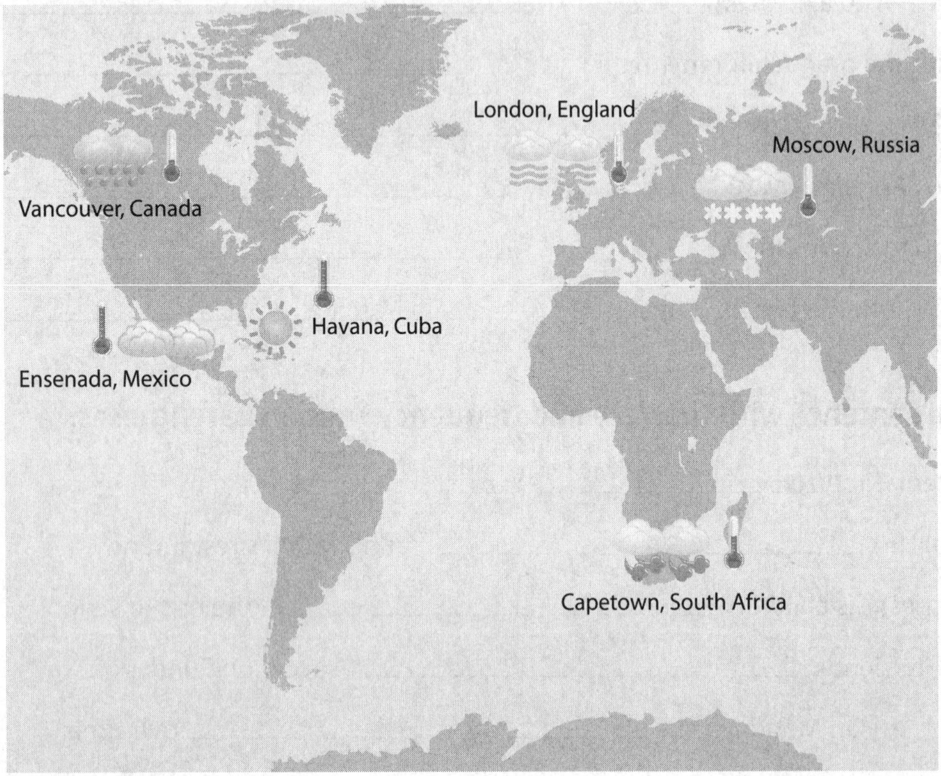

Vancouver, Canada: 1. *It's rainy and cold in Vancouver, Canada.*

Ensenada, Mexico: 2. ______________________________

Havana, Cuba: 3. ______________________________

London, England: 4. ______________________________

Moscow, Russia: 5. ______________________________

Capetown, South Africa: 6. ______________________________

B. Read the information below and write *sunny, rainy, cloudy, snowy, windy,* or *foggy* in the table. Then, write the temperatures.

This is WATV News giving you an update on this week's weather patterns.

Sunday: Today, it will be cloudy but warm. The low this Sunday morning is 32 degrees. The high will be 55 degrees.

Monday: Tomorrow, expect easterly winds at 10 miles per hour bringing in a cool, wet front.

Tuesday: On Tuesday, expect some precipitation. It will be rainy and between two and three inches will fall. The low will dip to about 36 degrees.

Wednesday: The following day will start foggy and the low will go below freezing, although the high will still be 55 degrees.

Thursday: It will be snowy on Thursday, perfect for winter sports.

5-Day Forecast									
Sunday		Monday		Tuesday		Wednesday		Thursday	
cloudy									
High:		**High:**	45°	**High:**	55°	**High:**		**High:**	35°
Low:		**Low:**	48°	**Low:**		**Low:**	28°	**Low:**	20°

C. Read the chart.

Yes/No Questions: *Is it?*				
			Answer	
Is it	Information	Question	Yes	No
Is it	hot windy cloudy rainy snowy cold foggy	**Is it** hot outside? **Is it** windy today? **Is it** cloudy in Florida? **Is it** rainy there? **Is it** snowy in the mountains? **Is it** cold in Chicago? **Is it** foggy in the morning?	Yes, **it is.**	No, **it isn't.**

D. Change the statements to questions.

1. It is rainy today.
   Is it rainy today? ____________________
2. It is snowy in the mountains and a beautiful day.
   ____
3. It is hot and 96 degrees in California today.
   ____
4. It is foggy by the ocean every morning.
   ____
5. It's windy at night.
   ____
6. It's cloudy and rainy today.
   ____

E. Read the weather forecast.

Sunday		Monday		Tuesday		Wednesday		Thursday	
sunny		windy		windy		cloudy		rainy	
High:	80º	**High:**	72º	**High:**	74º	**High:**	68º	**High:**	63º
Low:	65º	**Low:**	62º	**Low:**	60º	**Low:**	56º	**Low:**	52º

F. Answer the questions with short answers.

1. Today is Thursday. Is it sunny? No, it isn't.
2. Today is Sunday. Is the high 80 degrees? ____________________
3. Today is Tuesday. Is it windy? ____________________
4. Today is Sunday. Is it sunny? ____________________
5. It is Monday. Is the low 60 degrees? ____________________
6. Today is Wednesday. Is it cloudy? ____________________

G. Write two true statements about the weather today and two false statements.

True: ____________________

True: ____________________

False: ____________________

False: ____________________

PRACTICE TEST

A. Read and circle the correct answers.

Omar is a student at Alton Adult School. He is tall and thin. He has brown hair and brown eyes. He is 18 years old. Omar goes to school three times a week: Monday, Wednesday, and Friday. He works on the weekends from 7:00 a.m. to 5:00 p.m. He takes a lunch break at 11:30 a.m. Omar works outside, so he can't work when it rains. Usually it is sunny and about 80 degrees where he works.

1. When does Omar work?
   a. during the week
   b. on Saturdays and Sundays
   c. Monday, Wednesday, and Friday
   d. Omar doesn't work.

2. How's the weather when he works?
   a. It never rains.
   b. It rains a lot.
   c. It is usually sunny and about 80 degrees.
   d. It is cloudy all the time.

3. What do you think Omar's job is?
   a. He is an office worker.
   b. He works in a factory.
   c. He is a landscaper and works on people's yards.
   d. He is a doctor.

4. Which statement is true about Omar?
   a. He is short and thin.
   b. He has brown hair and green eyes.
   c. He works in the rain.
   d. He goes to school during the week.

B. Look at the picture and circle the correct answers.

1. Who is the tallest?
   a. Lien
   b. Anya
   c. Sung
   d. Marie

2. Which statement is true about the class?
   a. Dalva is taller than Sung.
   b. Gilberto is shorter than Sung.
   c. Marie is taller than Mario.
   d. Anya is younger than Kenji.

UNIT 2

LESSON 1 Shopping for clothes

GOAL ■ Identify clothing

A. Read the story about Gabriela and underline the clothing vocabulary.

Gabriela lives in Florida. She is new to the United States. She arrived with lots of winter clothes. She has sweaters and coats. She also has boots for the snow. But in Florida, it rarely snows. It's warm during winter months, so she needs some new clothes. She needs sandals and shorts. She also needs a few t-shirts. She lives near the ocean where people often wear very casual clothes.

B. Complete the sentences with words from the paragraph.

1. People wear ______________________ in the snow to keep their feet dry and warm.
2. Some people wear ______________________ when it is cold. They are usually not heavy like coats.
3. Many people wear ______________________ in the summer. They don't wear long pants.
4. ______________________ don't have long sleeves and usually don't have buttons.
5. In the summer, many people wear ______________________. They don't wear boots.

C. **Read the clothing words.**

sandals	scarf	shorts	boots
t-shirt	jacket	sweater	sunglasses
cap	dress	coat	swimsuit

D. **Complete the diagram with the words from Exercise C.**

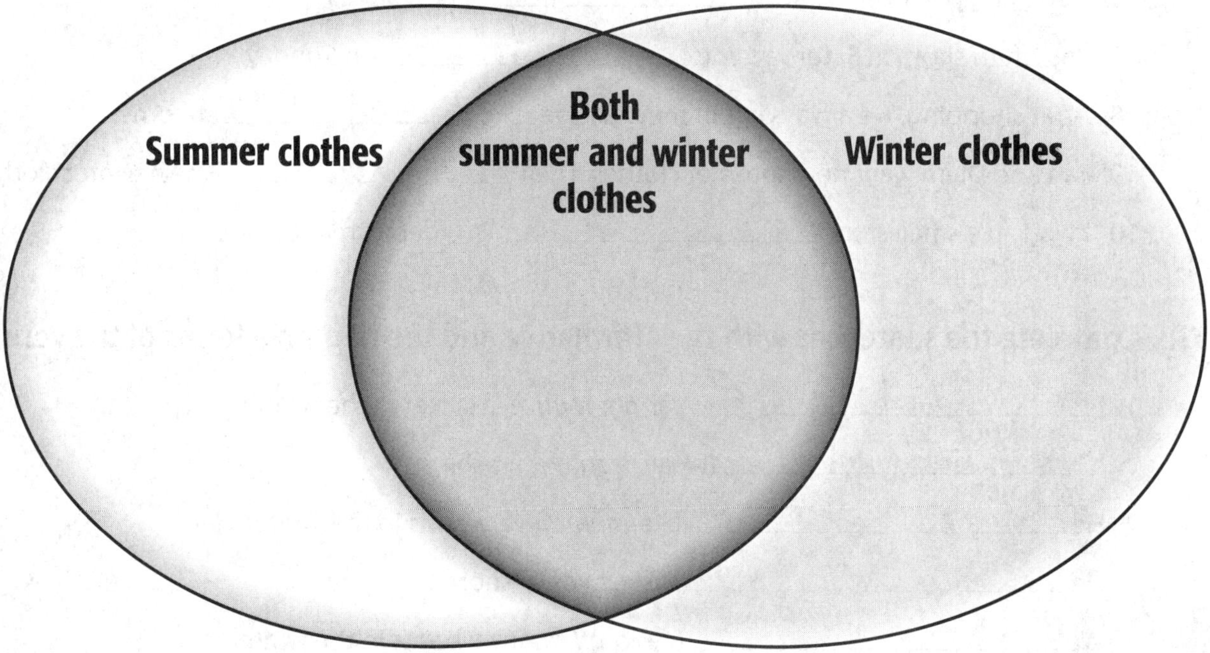

E. **Read the charts.**

Affirmative Simple Present		
I You We They	**wear** **like** **want** **need**	shoes.
He She	**wears** **likes** **wants** **needs**	

Negative Simple Present			
I You We They	**do not** **(don't)**	**wear** **like** **want** **need**	sandals.
He She	**does not** **(doesn't)**		

F. Complete each sentence with the negative form of the underlined verb.

1. Kenji shops at Bayview Mall. He ___doesn't shop___ at Maple Lake Mall.
2. Marie wears sandals to the beach. She ______________ sandals to work.
3. I need jeans for work. I ______________ a suit.
4. You buy shoes at Allen's Shoe Store. You ______________ shoes at The Shoe Place.
5. My parents like the new mall. They ______________ the old mall.
6. Ivan needs new boots. He ______________ new shoes.
7. You often shop on Saturday. You ______________ on Sunday.
8. After shopping, we always eat in the mall. We ______________ at home.
9. Tan and Diem want new summer clothes. They ______________ new winter clothes.
10. I work in a small store. I ______________ in a department store.

G. Complete the sentences with the affirmative and the negative forms of the verbs.

1. I ___wear___ (wear-*affirmative*) a jacket in the winter.
   I ___don't wear___ (wear-*negative*) a t-shirt.
2. He ______________ (like-*affirmative*) a scarf in the winter.
   He ______________ (like-*negative*) shorts.
3. We ______________ (need-*affirmative*) boots in the winter.
   We ______________ (need-*negative*) sandals.
4. She ______________ (want-*affirmative*) shorts in the summer.
   She ______________ (want-*negative*) pants.
5. You ______________ (wear-*affirmative*) a jacket in the winter.
   You ______________ (wear-*negative*) a swimsuit.

H. Complete the table with clothing you wear at home and at work.

Home		Work	

UNIT 2

LESSON 2 How much is it?

GOAL ■ Ask about prices

A. Read the sentences and write the prices from the box next to the clothing items.

1. The coat is more expensive than the dress.
2. The shoes and the sneakers are the same price.
3. The scarf is cheaper than the pajamas.
4. The shirt is more expensive than the pajamas and cheaper than the belt.
5. The blouse is $29.95.
6. The skirt is more expensive than the blouse and cheaper than the pants.
7. How much is the jacket?

$15.95	~~$20.75~~	$29.95	$42.50
~~$18.50~~	$22.50	$32.00	~~$69.95~~
$18.99	$22.50	~~$33.99~~	$89.50

belt $20.75

blouse ____________

coat ____________

dress $69.95

jacket ____________

pajamas $18.50

pants $33.99

scarf ____________

shirt ____________

shoes ____________

skirt ____________

sneakers ____________

B. Read the price for each item and answer the questions.

1. How much is the dress? ______________________
2. How much are the shoes, the jacket, and the shirt together? ______________________
3. How much are the dress and the shirt together? ______________________
4. How much are the socks and shoes together? ______________________

C. Put the clothing from Exercise B in order from the cheapest to the most expensive.

cheapest ——————————————————————→ **most expensive**

socks ________ ________ ________ ________ ________

D. Read the chart.

Adjective	Comparative adjective	Example sentence
cheap	**cheaper**	The shirt is **cheaper** *than* the dress.
expensive	**more expensive**	The shoes are **more expensive** *than* the shirt.
	less expensive	The dress is **less expensive** *than* the jacket.
Adjective	**Superlatives**	**Example sentence**
cheap	**cheapest**	The socks are the **cheapest**.
expensive	**most expensive**	The jacket is the **most expensive**.
	least expensive	The socks are the **least expensive**.

E. Read the price tags and complete the sentences with the comparative or the superlative.

1. The pants are ______ *cheaper than* ______ the sweater.
2. The shorts are ____________________ the sandals.
3. The sweater is ____________________ the pajamas.
4. The pants are ____________________ the sandals.
5. The sandals are the ____________________.
6. The sweater is the ____________________.
7. The sandals and the shorts together are ____________________ than the sweater.
8. The pajamas and the sandals together are ____________________ the sweater and the pants.

F. Put the clothing from exercises B and E in order from the cheapest to the most expensive.

cheapest ————————————————→ **most expensive**

socks									

G. Look at the clothing in exercises B and E. Complete the sentences.

1. The sweater is cheaper than ____________________.
2. ____________________ are each more expensive than a dress.
3. ____________________ are the least expensive.
4. ____________________ is the most expensive.
5. ____________________ are less expensive than the ____________________.
6. ____________________ are cheaper than ____________________.

UNIT 2

LESSON 3 What are they wearing?

GOAL ■ Describe clothing

A. Read the inventory and answer the questions.

Item number	Size	Color / Pattern	Item	Retail unit price	Quantity
015534-B	S	blue	short-sleeved shirt	$24.50	28
015534-W	S	white	short-sleeved shirt	$24.50	15
015655-B	S	blue/striped	long-sleeved shirt	$24.50	18
025533-Br	M	brown	long-sleeved shirt	$44.98	2
025531-B	M	blue/flowered	long-sleeved shirt	$32.95	31
035573-Br	L	brown	short-sleeved shirt	$35.75	7
045521-G	XL	green	short-sleeved shirt	$45.99	5

1. How many blue, short-sleeved shirts are in stock? ____________________
2. How many flowered shirts are in stock? ____________________
3. How many long-sleeved shirts are in stock? ____________________
4. How many extra-large shirts are in stock? ____________________
5. What size are the white shirts? ____________________
6. What size are the shirts for $44.98? ____________________
7. What color are the large shirts? ____________________
8. What color are the extra-large shirts? ____________________

B. Look at the inventory again. Make calculations.

1. How much is it for three small shirts? ____________________
2. How much is it for one medium brown shirt and the white shirt? ____________________
3. How much is it for two green shirts? ____________________
4. How much is it for three striped shirts? ____________________

C. Look at Lien and Steve and complete the sentences.

Lien Steve

1. Lien is wearing ______________________ to keep her feet warm.
2. ______________________ is wearing sandals.
3. Lien is wearing a ______________________ around her neck.
4. ______________________ is wearing a ______________________ on his head.

D. Read the charts.

<table>
<tr><th colspan="4">Affirmative Present Continuous</th></tr>
<tr><th>Subject</th><th>Be</th><th>Base + ing</th><th></th></tr>
<tr><td>I</td><td>am</td><td rowspan="3">wearing
buying
going
shopping
eating</td><td>right now</td></tr>
<tr><td>You, We, They</td><td>are</td><td>at this moment</td></tr>
<tr><td>He, She, It</td><td>is</td><td>today</td></tr>
</table>

<table>
<tr><th colspan="5">Negative Present Continuous</th></tr>
<tr><th>Subject</th><th>Be</th><th>Not</th><th>Base + ing</th><th></th></tr>
<tr><td>I</td><td>am</td><td>not</td><td rowspan="3">waiting
buying
going
shopping
eating</td><td>right now</td></tr>
<tr><td>You, We, They</td><td>are</td><td>not (aren't)</td><td>at this moment</td></tr>
<tr><td>He, She, It</td><td>is</td><td>not (isn't)</td><td>today</td></tr>
</table>

E. Fill in the missing part of each sentence.

1. It's rain ing__________ today.
2. Marie isn't work __________ today.
3. She __________ going with us.
4. I'm wear __________ my raincoat.
5. We __________ wearing hats.
6. Anya and Ivan __________ shopping today.
7. They __________ buying winter clothes.
8. Mario __________ working today.
9. Teresa is work __________ right now.
10. They __________ n't going to the mall.

F. Use the words to write sentences in the present continuous.

EXAMPLE: many people / shop / today ______Many people are shopping today.______

1. I / buy / sandals ____________________
2. you / wear / your new blouse ____________________
3. three men / sit / on a bench ____________________
4. we / not / eat / at the mall today ____________________
5. Duong / go / to the shoe store ____________________
6. the children / talk / to their friends ____________________
7. Irina / not / buy the blue skirt ____________________
8. you / read / a book at the bookstore ____________________
9. we / take / the bus home ____________________

G. Write more sentences about Lien and Steve in Exercise C.

Lien ____.

Steve ____.

Lien ____.

Steve ____.

UNIT 2

LESSON 4 Advertisements

GOAL Read advertisements and receipts

A. Read the ads and complete the table.

Abel's Clothes for Men

Men's Shirts
Regular: $33.00
Sale: $28.00

Good from January 1st–January 31st

Men's Shoes
(January 15th only)

All $26.00
(Regular: $36.00)

Come to our blowout sale and see the great deals!

Abel's Clothes for Men
All ties and belts on sale!
Unbeatable prices!

Only $8.00 all day
Regular: $15.00

Saturday, January 15th

Elegant Suits

Sale Price: $289.00
Save $50

One suit per customer

(Jan 1st—Jan 31st)

Save $10!

Slacks
Many colors and all sizes

$38.95

January only

We have everything you need to walk tall!

Socks
Regular: $10.00
Sale Price: $6.00

January 1st—January 31st

	Regular price	Sale price	Savings	Date of sale
Shirts	$33.00		$5.00	January 1st-31st
Shoes				
Ties and belts				
Suits				
Slacks				
Socks				

B. Read the graph.

C. Answer the questions about the graph in Exercise B.

1. Where is it cheaper to buy women's shoes? ______________________________
2. Where is it cheaper to buy women's belts? ______________________________
3. Where is it more expensive to buy handbags? ______________________________
4. Where is it more expensive to buy women's shoes? ______________________________
5. Where is it more expensive to buy dresses? ______________________________

D. Estimate the prices for the graph in Exercise B.

	Shoes	Dresses	Handbags	Belts
Armstrong Clothing	$35.00			
Fashion Express	$39.00			

E. Read the chart.

Using *Because*			
		Reason	
Statement	*Because*	Subject + verb	Example sentence
I want the blue shirt	because	it is cheaper	I want the blue shirt **because** it is cheaper.
I shop at Addy's	because	it is close	I shop at Addy's **because** it is close to my home.
You like the shirt	because	it is green	You like the shirt **because** it is green.

F. Match the statement with the reason.

1. I like the blouses. — c
2. I want the dress.
3. I like the shoes.
4. I want the hat.
5. I like the shirt.
6. I want the pants.

a. The dress (It) is long and beautiful.
b. The shoes (They) are cheap.
c. The blouses (They) are cheaper than at Fashion Express.
d. The pants (They) are my size.
e. The shirt (It) has long sleeves.
f. The hat (It) is perfect with my dress.

G. Combine the statements and the reasons in Exercise F with *because*.

1. I like the blouses because they are cheaper than at Fashion Express.
2. ________________
3. ________________
4. ________________
5. ________________
6. ________________

H. Read the paragraph.

Kim shops at Sally's Clothing Store because it has good prices. The store has good salespeople. Sally's Clothing Store has a great selection for women. The store is downtown on First and Main. Kim likes the shoes. They are cheaper than at other stores.

I. Write sentences using *because* to answer the questions.

1. Why does Kim like Sally's Clothing Store?
   Kim likes Sally's Clothing Store because it has good prices.
2. What is another reason she likes the store? (good salespeople)
   ____
3. What is another reason she likes the store? (great selection)
   ____
4. Why does Kim like the shoes?
   ____

UNIT 2

LESSON 5 Which one do you want?

GOAL ■ Ask for assistance

A. Read the conversation and answer the questions.

Salesperson: Can I help you?

Erica: Yes, I have a problem. These shoes are very uncomfortable. I think they are too small. Can I get a refund?

Salesperson: Do you have a receipt?

Erica: No, I'm sorry. Can I exchange them?

Salesperson: I think that's OK.

Erica: Thank you. Now, about this blouse.

Salesperson: You have another exchange?

Erica: Yes, this is damaged. You see here—it's torn.

Salesperson: Let me talk to the manager.

1. What are the two problems? ______________________________
2. Does Erica have a receipt? ______________________________
3. Can she get a refund? ______________________________

B. Identify the problems in the statements below. Use the ideas in the box.

I don't like the color.	It is damaged. / They are damaged.
It doesn't fit. / They don't fit.	

1. Excuse me. Can I exchange this? It is too big.

   Problem: ______________________________

2. Excuse me. I want to return this blouse. I want green not white.

   Problem: ______________________________

3. I need to return these shoes. They hurt my feet.

   Problem: ______________________________

4. This belt is broken. It doesn't buckle.

   Problem: ______________________________

5. These socks are torn. Can I please return them?

   Problem: ______________________________

C. Read the information. Choose a person and write a conversation like the one below.

I don't like the color.	It doesn't fit. (They don't fit.)
I don't like it. (I don't like them.)	It is the wrong size. (They are the wrong size.)
It is damaged. (They are damaged.)	

1. **Roberto**
   Item: these jeans
   Problem: size
2. **Gilberto**
   Item: this shirt
   Problem: color
3. **Janet**
   Item: these shoes
   Problem: color
4. **Marie**
   Item: this dress
   Problem: damaged
5. **Lien**
   Item: these socks
   Problem: damaged
6. **Alexi**
   Item: these shorts
   Problem: size

Manager: May I help you?

Roberto: Yes, I want to return these jeans.

Manager: OK, what's the problem?

Roberto: They don't fit.

Manager: ______________________________

________: ______________________________

Manager: ______________________________

________: ______________________________

D. Read the chart.

Demonstrative Adjectives: *This, That, These, Those*		
	Near	Far
Singular	**this** sweater **this** hat	**that** sweater **that** hat
Plural	**these** shoes **these** pants	**those** shoes **those** pants

Example Sentences		
	Near	Far
Singular	**This** sweater is perfect. I want **this** hat.	**That** sweater is blue. I like **that** hat.
Plural	I like **these** shoes. **These** pants fit.	I like **those** shoes. **Those** pants are great!

E. Read each sentence. Are the underlined words *singular* or *plural, near* or *far*? Check (✓) two boxes for each sentence.

	Singular	Plural	Near	Far
1. <u>Those apples</u> are delicious.	☐	☑	☐	☑
2. Are <u>those belts</u> expensive?	☐	☐	☐	☐
3. How much is <u>that t-shirt</u>?	☐	☐	☐	☐
4. What color are <u>these ties</u>?	☐	☐	☐	☐
5. Is <u>that dress</u> new?	☐	☐	☐	☐
6. <u>These apples</u> are green.	☐	☐	☐	☐
7. <u>This vacuum cleaner</u> is heavy.	☐	☐	☐	☐
8. I don't like <u>those jeans</u>.	☐	☐	☐	☐

F. Use *this, that, these, those,* and the information in parentheses to complete the sentences.

1. (near) Look at ______this______ shirt. It's perfect for school.
2. (near) I want to return ________________ shoes. They don't fit.
3. (far) ________________ pants are the wrong size.
4. (near) I like ________________ scarf. It's beautiful.
5. (far) ________________ shorts are very colorful.
6. (far) ________________ socks are not my size.
7. (near) I want to return ________________ radio.
8. (far) ________________ books are interesting.
9. (far) ________________ cars are new.
10. (near) We need ________________ gloves for the winter.

G. You need to return some things to the store. Write a conversation.

Manager: ____

Customer: ____

Manager: ____

Customer: ____

Manager: ____

Customer: ____

PRACTICE TEST

A. Circle the correct answers.

1. What is the regular price for shirts?
   a. $19.50 b. $2.00
   c. $17.50 d. on sale
2. What is the sale price for coats?
   a. $5.00 b. cheap
   c. expensive d. $44.50
3. Do they have small blouses?
   a. yes b. maybe
   c. no d. I don't know.

B. Circle the correct answers.

Lana's BOUTIQUE

Women's boots	$32.55
Women's pants	$24.50
Belt	$18.95
Blouse	$32.50
TOTAL	$108.50

Clothing for Less

Women's boots	$28.55
Women's pants	$30.00
Belt	$12.95
Blouse	$28.50
TOTAL	$100.00

Customer Copy

THE TRUE Shopper

Women's boots	$40.00
Women's pants	$34.00
Belt	$24.50
Blouse	$26.95
TOTAL	$125.45

No Refunds without Receipt

1. Where are boots the cheapest?
   a. Lana's b. Clothing for Less
   c. The True Shopper d. belts at Clothing for Less
2. Where are belts the least expensive?
   a. Lana's b. Clothing for Less
   c. The True Shopper d. They are all expensive.

UNIT 3

LESSON 1 Augustin's Restaurant

GOAL ■ Read a menu

A. Read the menu and answer the questions.

Edgar's Kitchen

SOUPS AND SALADS

Split pea soup	$1.99
Wonton soup	$1.99
Caesar salad	$2.49
Dinner salad	$1.99

SIDE ORDERS

French fries	$1.49
Potato chips	$.99
Onion rings	$1.49
Baked potato	$1.25

SANDWICHES

Ham and cheese	$3.99
Tuna	$3.99
Roast beef	$4.29
Hamburger	$3.49

MAIN DISHES

Roast beef with whipped potatoes and vegetables	$7.49
Teriyaki chicken with rice and vegetables	$5.99
Beef and broccoli with fried rice	$4.99
Sirloin steak with a baked potato and vegetables	$8.99

DESSERTS

Vanilla ice cream	$2.49
Carrot cake	$2.49
Apple pie	$2.49

BEVERAGES

Soda	$.99
Milk	$1.29
Coffee	$1.29
Tea	$1.29

1. Which is the most expensive item on the menu? sirloin steak with a baked potato and vegetables
2. Which are the cheapest items on the menu? ______________________
3. Which is your favorite sandwich on the menu? ______________________
4. Which is your favorite main dish on the menu? ______________________

B. Read the menu and make calculations.

1. What is the total for a dinner salad, a sirloin steak with a baked potato and vegetables, and a milk? __________
2. What is the total for a split pea soup, a ham and cheese sandwich, and a soda? __________
3. What is the total for a Caesar salad and a tuna sandwich? __________
4. What is the total for a dinner salad, beef and broccoli with fried rice, and a tea? __________
5. What is the total for a roast beef sandwich, a soda, and apple pie? __________
6. What is the total for a Caesar salad and a tea? __________

C. Look at the menu in Exercise A and read the conversations below. Complete the orders.

1.

Server: Are you ready to order?

Customer: Yes, thank you. I would like a Caesar salad and a tuna sandwich, please.

Server: OK. And to drink?

Customer: A lemon-lime soda, please.

Server: That's a Caesar salad, a tuna sandwich, and a soda. Coming right up.

Edgar's Kitchen *Order*	
Total	

2.

Server: May I take your order?

Customer: Yes. I would like the sirloin steak with a baked potato and vegetables.

Server: Would you like the steak cooked medium?

Customer: Yes. And coffee to drink.

Server: Fine. A sirloin steak and coffee.

Edgar's Kitchen *Order*	
Total	

D. Read the chart.

<table>
<tr><th colspan="4">Questions with Can</th></tr>
<tr><th>Can</th><th>Subject</th><th>Base verb</th><th>Example sentence</th></tr>
<tr><td>Can</td><td>I</td><td rowspan="2">take
help</td><td>Can I take your order?
Can I help you?</td></tr>
<tr><td>Can</td><td>you</td><td>Can you take my order?
Can you take our order, please?
Can you help me?
Can you help us?</td></tr>
</table>

E. Write questions with the words provided.

1. I / can / take / your dishes Can I take your dishes?
2. help / me / understand / can / you ______
3. you / see / can / the server ______
4. you / can / eat / faster ______
5. I / can / talk to the manager ______
6. pay / can / you ______
7. I / have / can / the shrimp ______
8. help / you / can ______

F. Match each statement with a question.

1. I need the server.	a. Can I have the dinner salad?
2. I want the dinner salad.	b. Can I speak to the manager?
3. I need the manager!	c. Can you see the server?
4. I finished my dinner.	d. Can I take your dishes?

G. Read the statements and write questions.

1. I want a soda. Can I have a soda, please?
2. I want to talk to the manager. ______
3. You need to help me. ______
4. You can take my dishes. ______

H. Look at the menu in Exercise A. Complete the order form and write a conversation. See Exercise C for help.

Edgar's Kitchen Order	
Total	

Server: ______

You: ______

Server: ______

You: ______

Server: ______

UNIT 3

LESSON 2 Do we need carrots?

GOAL ■ Make a shopping list

A. Read the advertisement and complete the table.

Product	Container or quantity	Price
	each	$.99
		$.60
		$3.40
spaghetti		
		$3.25
	six-pack cans	
		$3.20
	one-pound package	

B. Look at the shopping lists and complete the Venn diagram.

Jose

3 pounds of bananas
2 gallons of milk
1 loaf of bread
1 jar of peanut butter
2 boxes of cereal
3 bags of potato chips

Marie

2 pounds of oranges
1 can of green beans
1 loaf of bread
2 gallons of milk
1 carton of ice cream
1 bottle of oil

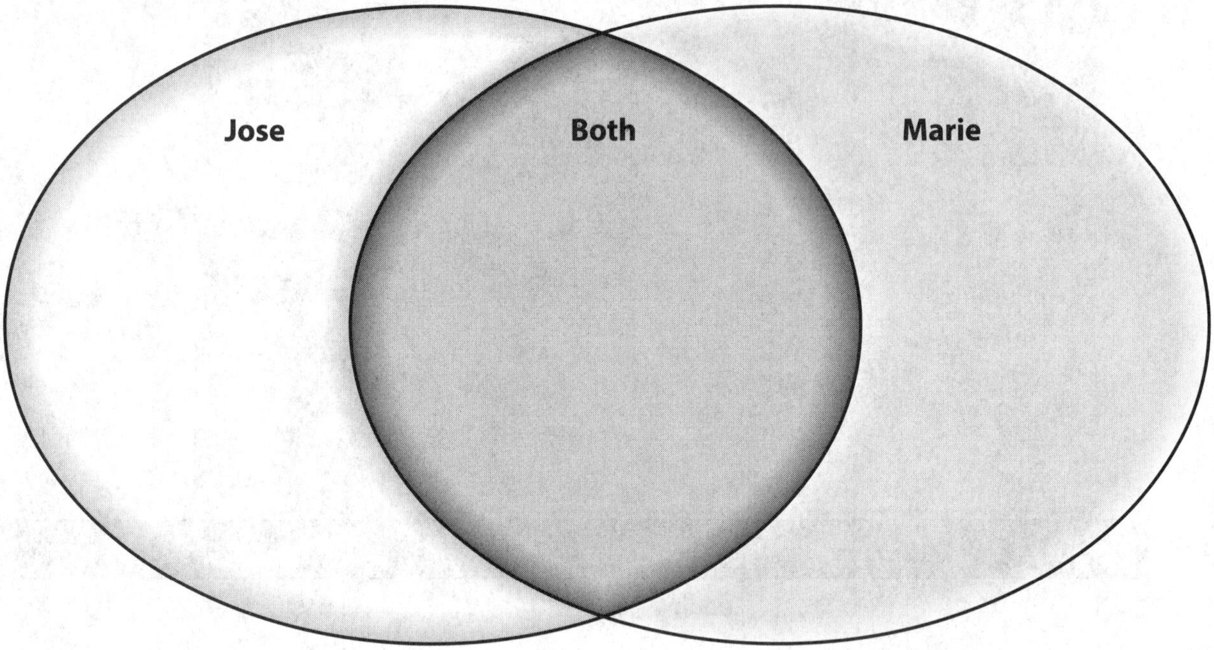

C. Read the chart.

How much / How many	
Count nouns	**Noncount nouns**

Use *many* with nouns you can count.	Use *much* with nouns you cannot count.
Example questions	
How many tomatoes do we need? **How many** pounds of tomatoes do we need?	**How much** flour do we need? **How much** rice do we need?

D. Put the words in the correct column.

~~bottles of water~~	oil	ice cream	cartons
gallons of milk	jars	milk	soup
cans of soup	water	pounds of potatoes	bread

How much	*How many*
	bottles of water

E. Write questions about the lists in Exercise B.

1. How many pounds of bananas do we need ?
2. How much ______________________________?
3. How much ______________________________?
4. How many ______________________________?
5. How many ______________________________?
6. How much ______________________________?
7. How many ______________________________?
8. How much ______________________________?
9. How much ______________________________?
10. How many ______________________________?

F. You are having a party for 50 people. What do you need? Make a shopping list on a separate piece of paper.

UNIT 3

LESSON 3 At the supermarket

GOAL ■ Locate items in a supermarket

A. **Look at the supermarket aisles in the pictures. Complete the table by listing two or more items you might expect to find in each aisle.**

Aisle 1: Produce	Aisle 4: Baking Needs	Aisle 8: Meats
pears, oranges, tomatoes		
Aisle 3: Canned Goods	**Aisle 5: Dairy/Frozen Foods**	

B. **Write sentences with your information from Exercise A.**

EXAMPLE: *The pears are in the produce aisle.*

1. ______________________________

2. ______________________________

3. ______________________________

4. ______________________________

5. ______________________________

6. ______________________________

C. Read the chart.

Answers with *Be*		
Subject	*Be*	Location
The milk It	**is**	in Aisle 1.
The eggs They	**are**	in Aisle 5.

D. Write sentences using subject pronouns with the given information. Use the pictures in Exercise A to help you.

1. **bananas:** The bananas are in the produce aisle. They are in Aisle 1.
2. **ham:** ______________________________
3. **milk:** ______________________________
4. **green beans:** ______________________________
5. **eggs:** ______________________________
6. **cake mix:** ______________________________

E. Read the chart.

Questions with *Be*		
Question word	*Be*	Singular or plural
Where	**is**	the milk? the water? the oil?
Where	**are**	the eggs? the bananas? the pears?

E. Check (✓) the correct form.

1. Where ______________ the potato chips? ☐ is ☑ are
2. Where ______________ the soup? ☐ is ☐ are
3. Where ______________ the milk? ☐ is ☐ are
4. Where ______________ the bread? ☐ is ☐ are
5. Where ______________ the cake mix? ☐ is ☐ are
6. Where ______________ the oranges? ☐ is ☐ are
7. Where ______________ the chicken? ☐ is ☐ are
8. Where ______________ the cookies? ☐ is ☐ are
9. The peanut butter ______________ in Aisle 3. ☐ is ☐ are
10. The flour ______________ in Aisle 4. ☐ is ☐ are
11. The carrots ______________ in the produce section. ☐ is ☐ are
12. The bread ______________ in the bakery. ☐ is ☐ are

F. Use Exercise A to complete the missing questions and answers.

Questions	Answers
Where are the potatoes?	
Where is the cake mix?	
	The cheese is in Aisle 5.
Where are the pears?	
	The milk is in the dairy section.
Where is the flour?	
	The bread is in the bakery.
	The chicken is in the meat section.

G. Write a conversation using some of the information in Exercise F.

Student A: ______________________________

Student B: ______________________________

Student A: ______________________________

Student B: ______________________________

Student A: ______________________________

UNIT 3

LESSON 4 A healthy diet

GOAL ■ Identify healthy foods

A. Check (✓) the correct column for each food item.

Food items	Protein	Vegetables	Fruit	Grains	Dairy
apples			✓		
avocados					
bananas					
bread					
butter					
cheese					
eggs					
ground beef					
ham					
lettuce					
nuts					
oranges					
pineapples					
turkey					
tomatoes					

B. Check (✓) the item you should eat more.

1. ☐ eggs or ☐ butter
2. ☐ oranges or ☐ ground beef
3. ☐ lettuce or ☐ bread
4. ☐ bananas or ☐ cheese

C. Label the food groups with the words below.

grains	fruit	~~vegetables~~	dairy	protein

vegetables ____________________

____

____

____

____

D. Read the chart.

Using *Have*

Subject	*Have*	Information	Example sentence
I	have	cereal	I **have** cereal for breakfast.
You		pizza	You **have** pizza for dinner.
We		milk	We **have** milk with lunch.
They		eggs	They **have** eggs for breakfast.
He	has	soup	He **has** water with dinner.
She		ice cream	She **has** ice cream for dessert.

E. Write *have* or *has*.

1. John and Sylvia ___have___ cereal for breakfast.
2. Nathan and I ____________ steak for dinner.
3. You ____________ breakfast every morning.
4. They ____________ water with dinner every night.
5. I ____________ a salad for lunch and a sandwich for dinner.
6. Gilberto ____________ a piece of toast for breakfast.
7. She ____________ a hamburger every day for lunch.
8. He ____________ a donut for breakfast.

F. Read the information.

Javier	Huyen	Alexi
Breakfast: a donut, milk	**Breakfast:** cereal, milk	**Breakfast**: fruit, milk
Lunch: a ham sandwich	**Lunch:** a ham sandwich	**Lunch:** a hamburger, fries
Dinner: a salad, soda	**Dinner:** chicken and rice	**Dinner:** chicken and rice

G. Write sentences about the meals in Exercise F.

1. Javier ___has milk with a donut for breakfast___.
2. Huyen and Javier ________________________________.
3. Alexi ________________________________.
4. Alexi and Huyen ________________________________.
5. ________________________________
6. ________________________________
7. ________________________________
8. ________________________________

H. Complete the list of meals for yourself.

Breakfast: ________________________________

Lunch: ________________________________

Dinner: ________________________________

UNIT 3

LESSON 5 Following instructions

GOAL ■ Read recipes

A. Read the menu and underline the verbs.

RECIPE BOX | SHOPPING LISTS | MEAL PLANNER | COOKING SCHOOL   Sign In

Spaghetti and Meatballs

Ingredients: *Serves 6 people*

2 jars of tomato sauce
2 eggs
1 onion
1 package of spaghetti
2 pounds of ground beef
salt
pepper

Instructions:

1. Cook the pasta according to package directions.
2. Combine the eggs, chopped onion, salt, and pepper in a large bowl. Add the beef and mix well.
3. Shape the mixture into approximately 48 balls and fry until cooked.
4. Heat the tomato sauce for 10 minutes on medium heat.
5. Add the meatballs and simmer for 15 minutes. Then, add to pasta and serve.

Save Recipe | E-mail | Print |

B. Match the verbs to the ingredients. Draw lines.

add	mixture
combine	pasta
shape	tomato sauce
cook	eggs, onion, salt, and pepper
heat	beef

C. **Read the recipe.**

Egg Salad Sandwiches

		Serves 4 people
Ingredients	6 eggs	8 slices of bread
	2 tablespoons of mayonnaise	salt to taste
	1 tablespoon of mustard	
	lettuce	
Instructions	❶ Boil eggs.	
	❷	
	❸	
	❹	
	❺	
	❻	
	❼	
	❽	

D. **Read the instructions below. They are in the wrong order. Number them in the correct order and fill in the *Instructions* section on the recipe card in Exercise C.**

_____ Put eggs in cold water.

_____ Serve on bread.

__1__ Boil eggs.

_____ Finally, add salt and chopped lettuce.

_____ Mash eggs with a fork.

_____ Add mayonnaise and mustard.

_____ Peel eggs.

__6__ Mix ingredients.

E. **Read the charts.**

Imperatives		
	Base verb	**Example sentence**
~~you~~	drain	**Drain** the water.
	chop	**Chop** the potatoes.
	peel	**Peel** the potatoes.

Negative Imperative			
		Base verb	**Example sentence**
~~you~~	do not don't	boil	**Don't boil** the water.
		use	**Do not use** butter.
		cook	**Don't cook** in the microwave.

F. Complete each sentence with a verb from the box. Some verbs can be used more than once.

read	listen	don't put	~~help~~	write
don't use	don't eat	don't take	don't cook	cut

1. ____Help____ your sister make dinner.
2. ____________ the shopping list.
3. ____________ my bowl.
4. ____________ to your parents.
5. ____________ eggs in the microwave.
6. ____________ candy all day.
7. ____________ the carrots in half.
8. ____________ a check for the food.
9. ____________ the dog to the restaurant.
10. ____________ pennies in the vending machine.

G. Read Silvia's instructions to her children. Use the imperatives of the verbs in parentheses.

__Don't watch__ (watch, *negative*) TV now. I need your help. Please ____________ (1. vacuum) the rug and ____________ (2. clean) your rooms. ____________ (3. eat, *negative*) the snacks in the living room. ____________ (4. buy) eggs, milk, and bread. ____________ (5. buy, *negative*) the food at the convenience store. ____________ (6. go) to Food City. ____________ (7. peel) and ____________ (8. whip) the potatoes. ____________ (9. make) a salad. ____________ (10. wash) and ____________ (11. drain) the lettuce first. Then, ____________ (12. set) the table. ____________ (13. use, negative) the blue plates. Use the white plates. ____________ (14. choose) some pretty napkins. ____________ (15. put) on some nice clothes.

H. Write your favorite recipe on a separate piece of paper. Use imperatives in the instructions.

PRACTICE TEST

A. Read about Gabriel and circle the correct answers.

Gabriel is a cook. He works at his father's restaurant. He went to cooking school and can make many different kinds of food. Gabriel especially likes to make Italian food. He makes pasta himself and loves spaghetti. It is his favorite. He also loves making special salads with vegetables from his garden. Gabriel makes many kinds of soups, too. He hopes to have his own restaurant one day and cook international food. His father only has American food at his restaurant.

1. Where does Gabriel work?
   a. at an international restaurant
   b. at his father's restaurant
   c. at a restaurant that serves Chinese food
   d. at a cooking school
2. What does Gabriel like the most?
   a. hamburgers
   b. salads
   c. soups
   d. spaghetti
3. Where does Gabriel find some of his ingredients for his salads?
   a. at cooking school
   b. in his garden
   c. vegetables
   d. delicious foods

B. Read the recipe card and circle the correct answers.

Chocolate Peanut Candy

Dessert			Serves 6 people
Ingredients	12 oz. butterscotch chips		
	12 oz. chocolate chips		
	1 large can Spanish peanuts		
Instructions	Put butterscotch and chocolate chips in a pan and melt over low heat. Add peanuts. Drop one teaspoon at a time onto wax paper. Cool for three hours in the refrigerator.		

1. What is the container for the peanuts?
   a. large
   b. can
   c. Spanish
   d. one
2. How many people is this recipe for?
   a. 12
   b. 1
   c. 6
   d. 24

UNIT 4

LESSON 1 Looking for a place to live

GOAL ■ Describe housing

A. Read the information and complete the paragraph about Rosa.

Rosa Andrade
I live in a condominium.
It has three bedrooms.
It's on Adams Street.
I like my home.

Gilberto Leite
I live in an apartment.
It has one bedroom.
It's on Butcher Street.
I don't like my home. I want to move.

Rosa Andrade

My name is ______________. I am from Argentina. I live in Oakland, California now. I live in a ______________. It has ________ bedrooms. I live on ______________. I like my home.

B. Write a paragraph about Gilberto. He is from Brazil and lives in Miami, Florida.

Gilberto Leite

C. Read about Ahmed and answer the questions.

I lived in a small house in Oakland, California, but I needed more room. I wanted something with a bigger yard and four bedrooms. In the summer, I found a beautiful four-bedroom house, but the rent was high, and it was far from my work. The rent was $1,500 a month. I liked it so much that I decided to move in. I got a second job to pay the rent. I am happy in my new house, but I have to work a lot, so I am not there very much.

1. Why did Ahmed need a new house?
   a. He needed a bigger garage for his cars.
   (b.) His house was too small.
   c. He is happy in his new house.

2. How many bedrooms does the new house have?
   a. The rent is too high.
   b. It has four bedrooms.
   c. The rent is $1,500 a month.

3. Where is the house?
   a. It has a bigger yard.
   b. He found it in the summer.
   c. It is far from his work.

4. How can he afford his house?
   a. It's far from work.
   b. He got a second job.
   c. He works overtime.

D. Read the chart.

Information Questions with *Be* and *Do*			
Information word	***Be***	**Information**	**Example answer**
How much (money)	**is** **are**	the rent? the flowers?	$1,500 a month. $20.00.
Where	**is** **are**	the apartment? the apartments?	On First Street.
What kind of home **What kinds** of homes	**is** **are**	for rent? in the neighborhood?	An apartment. Apartments and houses.
Information word	***Do* + subject**	**Base verb**	**Example answer**
How much (money)	**do** you	**have?**	$20.00.
Where	**do** you	**live?**	On First Street.
What kind of home **What kinds** of homes	**do** you **do** you	**have?**	An apartment. Apartments and houses.
How many bedrooms	**does** it	**have?**	Three.

E. Check (✓) the correct answer.

1. How much ________ the cars?	☐ is	☑ are	☐ do you have
2. What furniture ________ in your apartment?	☐ is	☐ are	☐ do you
3. Where ________ sleep?	☐ is you	☐ are you	☐ do you
4. How many ________ do you have?	☐ car	☐ cars	☐ money
5. How much ________ need?	☐ is you	☐ are you	☐ do you
6. What kind of cars ________ in the garage?	☐ is	☐ are	☐ do you
7. What kind of sofa ________ need?	☐ is you	☐ are you	☐ do you
8. Where ________ the TV?	☐ is	☐ are	☐ do you

F. Match the question with the answer.

1. Where is the chair?	a. $175,000.
2. How much is the house?	b. A condominium.
3. Where do you live?	c. In the bedroom.
4. What kind of home is on Palm Avenue?	d. Three.
5. How many bedrooms do you have?	e. In Fullerton.

G. Answer the questions about yourself.

1. What kind of home do you have? ________________________________
2. Where do you go to school? ________________________________
3. How many brothers and sisters do you have? ________________________________
4. How many bedrooms does your home have? ________________________________

H. Write a paragraph about yourself. Use the paragraphs from exercises A and B for help.

LESSON 2 Finding a home

GOAL Interpret classified ads

A. Read the classified ads and complete the table.

1. With two bedrooms and two full bathrooms, this apartment is a great value at $1,200. It has a modern kitchen with new countertops and appliances. The bathrooms have been updated, and the bedrooms have large closets. The price includes heat, air-conditioning, and hardwood flooring. Call 555-3645 for a tour.
2. House for rent! This three-bedroom, two-bathroom home is nestled against the mountains in Provo, Utah. A beautiful fireplace adorns the spacious living room, and there is carpet in every room. It is a bargain at $2,000 a month. E-mail us at jackson.linda@ma1l.com.
3. This two-bedroom, two-bathroom condo is perfect for a young family. The price is right, and it has all the amenities you could want: a new kitchen, a beautiful view from the master-bedroom balcony, and a community pool! Don't pass up this opportunity to rent a perfect home at only $1,550 a month. Text or call 555-9673 today and ask for Karen.
4. This small, one-bedroom, one-bathroom apartment is perfect for a single person on the go. It is cheap and will meet all your needs. There are no frills or amenities, but it's only $800 a month. Be sure to contact us via e-mail at tbrannigan@ma1l.com.

Type	Bedrooms	Bathrooms	Amenities	Contact
apartment				
	three			
			pool	
				e-mail

B. Read the classified ads and answer the questions. Write the numbers of the ads.

1.
FOR RENT
3 bdrm, 2 bath apt, utils. pd, $1,025. Call Angela @ 555-9922.

2.
For Rent
1 bdrm, 1 bath condo, air, big yard, pets OK, deposit, $1,400/month, new appliances, nr. schools and park. Call Betty, 555-3311.

3.
FOR RENT
1 bath, 1 bd., perfect for first home, air, no pets, $900, pool. Sam, 555-3456.

4.
FOR RENT
House – nr. schools, new appliances, 4 bed, 2 bath, 2 story, big yard. Call 555-7711, Frank. $1,800/m.

5.
FOR RENT
3 bedroom, 2 bath condo, nr. park, furnished, fireplace. Ginger – 555-2311. $1,200.

6.
FOR RENT
2 bd, 2 bth mobile home near school, new carpet, good neighborhood. $1,200 rent. Call 555-9912.

Abbreviations		
A/C: air-conditioning air: air-conditioning ba: bath	bd: bedroom bdrm: bedroom condo: condominium	nr: near pd: paid utils: utilities

1. Which rental has new carpet? ____________________
2. Which rental has a fireplace? ____________________
3. Which rental costs $1,800 a month? ____________________
4. Which rental allows pets? ____________________

C. Read the chart.

<table>
<tr><th colspan="5">Information Questions with Which</th></tr>
<tr><th>Information word</th><th>Subject</th><th>Verb</th><th>Information</th><th>Example question</th></tr>
<tr><td rowspan="4">Which</td><td>house</td><td>has</td><td rowspan="2">three bedrooms
a pool
a fireplace
a big yard</td><td>Which house has three bedrooms?</td></tr>
<tr><td>houses</td><td>have</td><td>Which houses have three bedrooms?</td></tr>
<tr><td>house</td><td>is</td><td rowspan="2">on First Street
next to the park</td><td>Which house is on First Street?</td></tr>
<tr><td>houses</td><td>are</td><td>Which houses are on First Street?
Which houses are next to the park?</td></tr>
</table>

D. Use the words to write questions.

1. house / is / near my school / which Which house is near my school?
2. have / houses / which / two bathrooms ______
3. which / has / house / a balcony ______
4. houses / are / which / big ______
5. has / apartment / which / furniture ______
6. is / condo / which / expensive ______
7. car / which / in the garage / is ______
8. at 10:00 a.m. / which / starts / class ______

E. Answer the questions about the classified ads in Exercise B.

1. Which homes have two bathrooms? Homes 1, 4, 5, and 6 have two bathrooms.
2. Which homes are condominiums? ______
3. Which home has a pool? ______
4. Which homes is the cheapest? ______
5. Which home is the most expensive? ______
6. Which two-bedroom home is $1,200? ______

F. Read the classified ads and write questions with *which*. Use Exercise E as a model.

1. **For Rent**
1 bed, 1 bath, view, fireplace, pool, house near schools, a/c. Call 555-5672.

2. **FOR RENT**
2 bed, 2 bath, apt, util paid, gd neighborhood, nr schools. Call Frank 555-0923.

3. **FOR RENT**
5 bed, 3 bath hse, view, pool, 2-car garage, landscaping. Mollie 555-9898.

1. ______
2. ______
3. ______
4. ______
5. ______
6. ______

UNIT 4

LESSON 3 At the rental agency

GOAL ■ Complete a rental application

A. Read the paragraph and answer the questions.

Javier Aguilar is married and has three children. He works for Anchor Motors. He is a mechanic. His wife works there, too. She is a secretary. Javier is looking for a new place to live because he needs a bigger home for his family. Right now, he has an apartment in Santa Clara, California, but it is too small. It only has two bedrooms. Javier wants to move to a house with a yard. He needs a three- or four-bedroom house in the same city.

1. What is Javier's last name? ______________________
2. Where does he work? ______________________
3. Where does his wife work? ______________________
4. What is his wife's position at work? ______________________
5. How many children does he have? ______________________
6. What city does he want to move to? ______________________

B. Complete the telephone conversation using the information from Exercise A.

Javier: Hello, I'm looking for a ______________ in Santa Clara to rent.

Agent: How many ______________ do you need?

Javier: I need ______________ or ______________ ______________.

Agent: Where do you live now?

Javier: I live in an ______________ in Santa Clara.

Agent: Why do you want to move to a new home?

Javier: We need something bigger with a ______________.

Agent: Thank you for the information. I will see what I can find.

C. Complete the rental application with the information from the box.

Javier	2 years, 6 months	Santa Clara	(408) 555-2234	94801
97235 Artesia Place	CA	Mechanic	Anchor Motors	

RENTAL APPLICATION

Name: Aguilar (last) ______ (first) ______ (mi) Phone: (   )

Present Address: 334 W. Horton Blvd. Work Phone: (408) 555-7698

City: ______ State: CA Zip: 95050 How long? ______ (years, months)

Prior Address: ______

City: Richmond State: ______ Zip: ______

Employer: ______ Phone: (408) 555-2543

Position: ______ How long? 8 years, 3 months (years, months)

D. Read the chart.

Information question	Example answer
What is your name?	My name is Javier Aguilar.
Where do you live now?	I live in Santa Clara.
Where did you live before?	I lived in Richmond.
How long did you live there?	I lived there for eight years.
Who is your employer?	I work for Anchor Motors.
What is your position?	I am a mechanic.

E. Write questions based on the answers below.

1. My last name is Johnson. What is your last name?
2. My bank is Americana Bank. What ____________________?
3. I go to school in Santa Clara. Where ____________________?
4. I worked in Santa Clara for three years. How long ____________________?
5. My supervisor is John Carpenter. Who ____________________?
6. I lived in Monterey. Where ____________________?

F. Match each question to an answer.

1. Where did you study English?	a. Steve Hampson
2. How long did you study English?	b. 9976 West Broadway.
3. Who was your teacher?	c. At Palm City Adult School.
4. What is the address?	d. Four years.

G. Write a conversation with the questions and answers in Exercise E.

Agent: What is your last name?

Eric Johnson: ____________________

Agent: ____________________

Eric Johnson: ____________________

Agent: ____________________

Eric Johnson: ____________________

Agent: ____________________

Eric Johnson: ____________________

Agent: ____________________

Eric Johnson: ____________________

Agent: ____________________

Eric Johnson: ____________________

UNIT 4

LESSON 4 We need furniture!

GOAL Identify rooms and furniture

A. Look at the furniture and complete the table. Check (✓) the rooms the furniture belongs in. More than one room can be selected.

$850.89

$34.49

$369.89

$449.99

$875.00

$225.89

$275.99

$149.99

Item	Unit price	Living room	Bedroom	Dining room
couch	*$850.89*	✓		

B. Look at the picture. List the furniture and other items in the kitchen.

C. Read the chart.

Prepositions	
The ball is **in** the box. 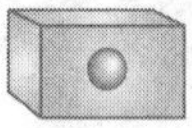	The ball is **between** two boxes. 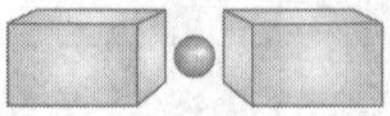
The ball is **on** the box. 	The ball is **over** the box. 
The ball is **under** the box. 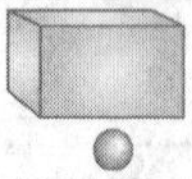	The ball is **in front of** the box. 
The ball is **next to** the box. 	The ball is **behind** the box. 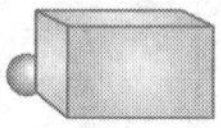
• Use prepositions to talk about where things are.	

D. Circle the most appropriate prepositions in each sentence.

1. The kitchen is **on / next to** the living room.
2. The microwave is **between / over** the stove.
3. The washer is **in the corner / in front of**.
4. The refrigerator is **next to / under** the stove.
5. The apples are **behind / in** the refrigerator.
6. The butter is **next to / in** the apples.
7. The sofa is **between / on** two windows.
8. The flowers are **in / on** the coffee table.
9. The book is **under / in** the armchair.
10. The TV is **under / in front of** the armchair.
11. The vacuum cleaner is **in / behind** the sofa.
12. The door is **between / over** the sofa and the chair.

E. Use the words to write sentences.

1. Madison Street / the house / is / on — The house is on Madison Street.
2. behind / the swimming pool / is / the house ____________________
3. the yard / of / is / in / the house / front ____________________
4. are / the corner / the flowers / in ____________________
5. is / the garage / next to / the house ____________________
6. over / the balcony / is / the door ____________________
7. in / is / the fireplace / the living room ____________________
8. between / the bathroom / is / two bedrooms ____________________
9. is / under / the dishwasher / the kitchen counter ____________________
10. over / the kitchen counter / the cupboard / is ____________________

F. Make a list of furniture and other items in your classroom.

1. clock
2. ____________
3. ____________
4. ____________
5. ____________
6. ____________

G. Write sentences about the locations of the items in your list in Exercise F.

1. The clock is on the wall.
2. ____________________
3. ____________________
4. ____________________
5. ____________________
6. ____________________

UNIT 4

LESSON 5 Family Budget

GOAL ■ Make a family budget

A. Plan your own budget.

1. What do you need every month?	Budget
food	$

2. What do you sometimes need to buy?	Budget
clothes	$

3. How much do you need for entertainment?	Budget
restaurants	$

4. How much do you want to put in savings?	Budget
savings	$

B. Read Alan's budget. Circle the items that are over budget and check the items that are under budget.

Alan's Budget		
MONTHLY INCOME: $5,467	Budget expenses	Actual expenses
Rent	$1,400	$1,400
Gas ✓	$50	$44
(Electric)	$140	$165
Water	$35	$31
Food	$1,000	$945
Life insurance	$105	$105
Gasoline	$250	$262
Phone bill	$175	$145
Entertainment	$400	$462
Clothing	$100	$76
Household repairs	$100	$24
Furniture	$100	$0
Savings	$1,000	$786
Other	$462	$872
TOTAL	**$5,317.00**	**$5,317.00**

C. Read the chart.

Modals: *May* and *Might* to Show Probability (Use Interchangeably)			
Subject	Modal	Base verb	Example sentence
I, You, He, She, It, We, They	may might	spend earn be	I **may** spend $250 on gasoline this month. You **may** spend $175 on the phone bill. He **may** earn $6,000. Food **might** be $1,000. We **may** earn $3,500 a month. They **may** spend $300 a month on food.

D. Rewrite the sentences with *may* to show probability.

1. We move in two weeks. We may move in two weeks.
2. They have a three-bedroom house. ______
3. She lives in an apartment on Main Street. ______
4. You need a new job. ______
5. It is a beautiful house. ______
6. He spends $300 a month. ______

E. Rewrite the sentences with *might* to show probability.

1. Gasoline is $250. Gasoline might be $250.
2. They need money for clothes. ______
3. She wants help with the rent. ______
4. He earns $6,500 a month. ______
5. We spend $800 on food. ______
6. I go to the bank today. ______

F. Complete the sentences about the budget in Exercise B.

1. He may spend $ 250 on gasoline.
2. He might spend $ ______ on furniture.
3. He might spend $ ______ on food.
4. He may spend $ ______ on the phone bill.
5. He might spend $ ______ on entertainment.
6. He may spend $ ______ on clothing.

PRACTICE TEST

A. Look at Ricardo's rental application and circle the correct answers.

RENTAL APPLICATION

① Phone ( ) ______

② Name Aguilar, Ricardo G. ______ Work Phone ( ) ______
last first mi

③ Present Address ______

④ City ______ State ______ Zip ______ How long? ______ months / years

⑤ Prior Address ______

⑥ City ______ State ______ Zip ______ How long? ______ months / years

⑦ Employer ______ Phone ( ) ______
How long? months / years

1. Which line is for Ricardo's address now?
   a. ② b. ③
   c. ⑤ d. ⑦

2. Which line is for his address before?
   a. ② b. ③
   c. ⑤ d. ⑦

3. Which line is for the company he works for?
   a. ② b. ⑤
   c. ⑦ d. ⑧

4. Which line is for his name?
   a. ② b. ⑤
   c. ⑦ d. ⑧

UNIT 5

LESSON 1 Getting around town

GOAL ■ Describe your community

A. Read the map and write *northwest, northeast, southwest, or southeast*.

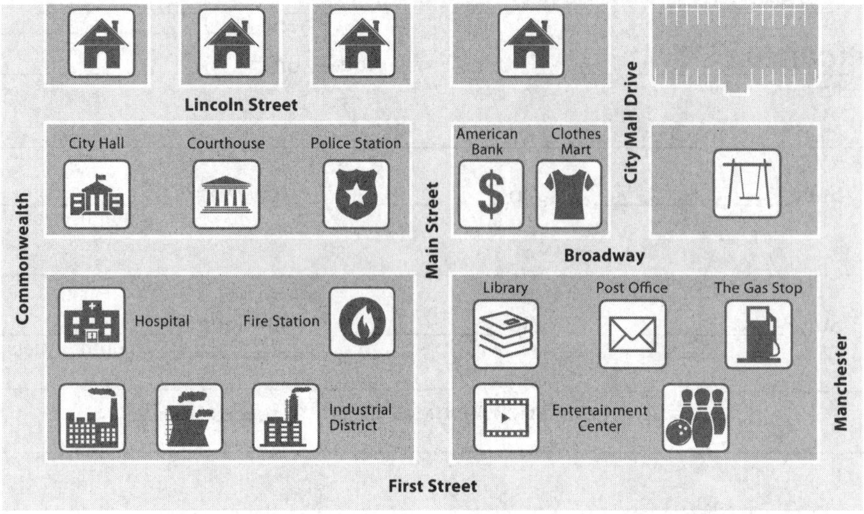

1. The parking lot is in the ______________________________.
2. The intersection of Commonwealth and Lincoln is in the ______________________________.
3. The bowling alley is in the ______________________________.
4. The factory is in the ______________________________.

B. Put the places in the box in the correct categories.

~~Circle Supermarket~~	Johnson Theaters	Milton's Fine Restaurant
Garden Apartments	Jay Manufacturing	Polly's Clothing Emporium
Country Golf Course	Reeds Electronics	Offices of Kirtland and Jones
Broadway Mobile Homes	Furniture Builders	Senior Living Residence

Shopping	Entertainment	Residential	Industry and business
Circle Supermarket			

C. Read the train schedule.

Train number	560	570	600	625
San Carlos	7:50 a.m.	9:50 a.m.	12:50 p.m.	2:20 p.m.
Palm City	8:02 a.m.	10:02 a.m.	1:02 p.m.	2:32 p.m.
Franklin City	8:19 a.m.	10:19 a.m.	1:19 p.m.	2:49 p.m.
Lakeview	8:34 a.m.	10:34 a.m.	1:34 p.m.	3:04 p.m.
Jackson	8:44 a.m.	10:44 a.m.	1:44 p.m.	3:14 p.m.
1. Main St	8:49 a.m.	10:49 a.m.	1:49 p.m.	3:19 p.m.
2. Broadway	8:54 a.m.	10:54 a.m.	1:54 p.m.	3:24 p.m.
3. N. Hart	9:00 a.m.	11:00 a.m.	2:00 p.m.	3:30 p.m.
Pleasantville	9:24 a.m.	11:24 a.m.	2:24 p.m.	3:54 p.m.
Casper	10:01 a.m.	12:01 p.m.	3:01 p.m.	4:31 p.m.

D. Answer the questions about the train schedule.

1. How long is the trip from Palm City to Lakeview? 32 minutes
2. How long is the trip from Pleasantville to Casper? __________
3. How long is the trip from San Carlos to Casper? __________
4. You want to arrive in Casper in the morning. Which train do you take? __________
5. You want to arrive in Casper around 3:00 p.m. Which train do you take? __________
6. You want to arrive in Casper after 4:30 p.m. Which train do you take? __________

E. Read the chart.

When, Where, and Prepositions			
	Base verb	Preposition	Example question
When does the bus	stop	**at** (street) **in** (a city)	**When** does the bus stop **at** Main Street? **When** does the bus stop **in** Casper?
	leave	Ø (no preposition) **for** (destination) **from** (start)	**When** does the bus leave Main Street? **When** does the bus leave **for** Casper? **When** does the bus leave **from** San Carlos?
	arrive	**from** (start) **at** (street) **in** (city)	**When** does the bus arrive **from** San Carlos? **When** does it arrive **at** Main Street? **When** does it arrive **in** Casper?
Where does the bus	stop	**in** (city)	**Where** does the bus stop **in** Jackson?

F. Circle the correct preposition.

1. When does the train stop (in) / **on** San Carlos?
2. Where does the bus stop **in** / **on** Pleasantville?
3. When does the train arrive **in** / **at** North Hart Street?
4. When does the bus leave **at** / Ø Pleasantville?
5. Where does the train stop **for** / **in** San Carlos?
6. When does the train arrive **for** / **in** Richmond?
7. When does the bus arrive **from** / Ø Los Angeles?
8. When does the train leave **for** / **in** Broadway?

G. Look at the schedule in Exercise C. Complete the sentences.

1. Train 600 arrives in ___Lakeview___ at 1:34 p.m.
2. Train 570 leaves for ______________ from Palm City at ______________.
3. Train 625 stops in ______________ at ______________ at 3:24 p.m.
4. Train 570 arrives from ______________ at 10:44 a.m.
5. Train 560 leaves ______________ at 9:24 a.m.
6. Train 625 stops at ______________ in ______________ at 3:24 p.m.

H. Write questions for the statements you completed in Exercise G.

1. When does Train 600 arrive in Lakeview?
2. ______________________________
3. ______________________________
4. ______________________________
5. ______________________________
6. ______________________________

UNIT 5

LESSON 2 What's the number?

GOAL ■ Scan an Internet search page

A. Look at the directory and complete the table.

COMMUNITY DIRECTORY

City Hall..555-7834
1285 W. Harbor Blvd.

Courthouse.......................................555-7845
1287 W. Harbor Blvd.

DMV *(Department of Motor Vehicles)*
Information...................................555-7777
Appointments 555-7778
92 W. Archer Blvd.

Schools *(Public)*
Alton Junior High...........................555-2964
34 Alton Parkway
Lincoln High...................................555-8336
278 Lincoln Ave
Washington Elementary..................555-5437
210 Washington St.

Fire Department...............................555-8461
Emergencies call 911
687 Broadway Ave.

Police Department............................555-7820
Emergencies call 911
1200 W. Harbor Blvd.

Playgrounds and Parks
Department of Parks
and Recreation................................555-8612
1295 Harbor Blvd.
Carlton Park
11278 Park Lane
Keaton Park
2 Ridge Route

Library *(Public)*................................555-1236
22 S. Banning Ave.

U. S. Post Office................................555-6245
151 E. Broadway

Need or problem	Agency name	Phone number
I need a driver's license.	DMV	555-7777 / 555-7778
I need to register for high school.		
A house is on fire.		
I want to borrow a book.		
I need to pick up a package.		
There is an emergency.		
I want to find a park nearby.		
I want to get a library card.		
I need to mail a letter.		

B. Read the paragraph and answer the questions.

Emma is a new student at the adult school. She is also new to Palm City. Emma needs to do many things as soon as possible. She needs to enroll her children in school. She needs to call the gas and electric companies to start service. She needs to go to the post office to give them her information for mail delivery. She needs a new job, too. Emma will look on the Internet for work. Maybe she can find information about the gas and electric companies there, too.

1. Write the sentence that tells you Emma has a new address.

____

2. Write the sentence that tells you Emma has children.

____

3. Write the sentence that tells you Emma probably has a computer.

____

4. Write the sentence that tells you Emma has no electricity in her house.

____

C. Read the chart.

Simple Present		
Subject	**Verb**	**Example sentence**
I, You, We, They	want need call look (for)	I **want** a new car. You **need** the number for the hospital. We **call** for assistance. They **look** for information in the directory.
He, She	wants needs calls looks (for)	He **wants** to mail a package. She **needs** a driver's license. He **calls** the courthouse every week. She **looks** for books.

D. Complete each sentence with the correct form of the verb in the simple present.

1. Kenji ___needs___ (need) the police immediately.
2. The women ____________ (call) the hospital every hour.
3. He ____________ (want) to mail a package to his mother in Colombia.
4. She ____________ (look) for places to have a picnic in the city directory.
5. We ____________ (call) the DMV when we buy a new car.
6. I ____________ (like) the doctor on Main Street.
7. She ____________ (prefer) to go to a park.
8. The nurse ____________ (call) the doctor every day.
9. We ____________ (eat) lunch at the restaurant on the corner.
10. The bus ____________ (stop) on the corner of Main and Nutwood.
11. I ____________ (visit) Marie on Saturdays.
12. My husband ____________ (come) with me to the hospital.

E. Use the simple present to write reasons why Raquel and Mario may call the places in parentheses.

1. (bank) Raquel needs money.
2. (dentist) Raquel ____________.
3. (shoe store) Raquel ____________.
4. (doctors) Raquel and Mario ____________.
5. (optometrist) Raquel ____________.
6. (hospital) Raquel and Mario ____________.
7. (DMV) Raquel ____________.
8. (fire department) Mario ____________.

F. Write reasons why you may call a restaurant, a bank, and a rental car agency.

1. (restaurant) ____________
2. (bank) ____________
3. (rental car agency) ____________

UNIT 5

LESSON 3 Finding your way

GOAL Give and follow directions

A. **Look at the map and complete the sentences with prepositions from the box. You can use the prepositions more than one time.**

next to	on the corner of
across from	on

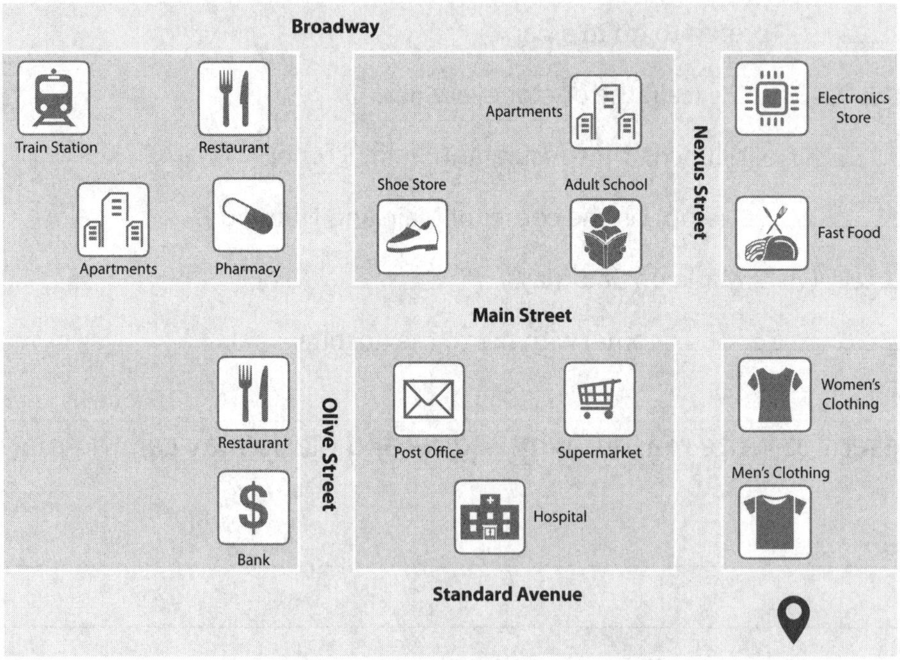

1. The electronics store is *on the corner of* Broadway and Nexus Street.
2. The women's clothing store is ______________ the men's clothing store.
3. The hospital is ______________ Standard Avenue.
4. The bank is ______________ Olive Street and Standard Avenue.
5. The adult school is ______________ the shoe store.
6. The train station is ______________ Broadway.
7. The pharmacy is ______________ the shoe store.
8. The post office is ______________________________.
9. The apartments are ______________________________.
10. The train station is ______________________________.

B. Look at the map and follow the directions.

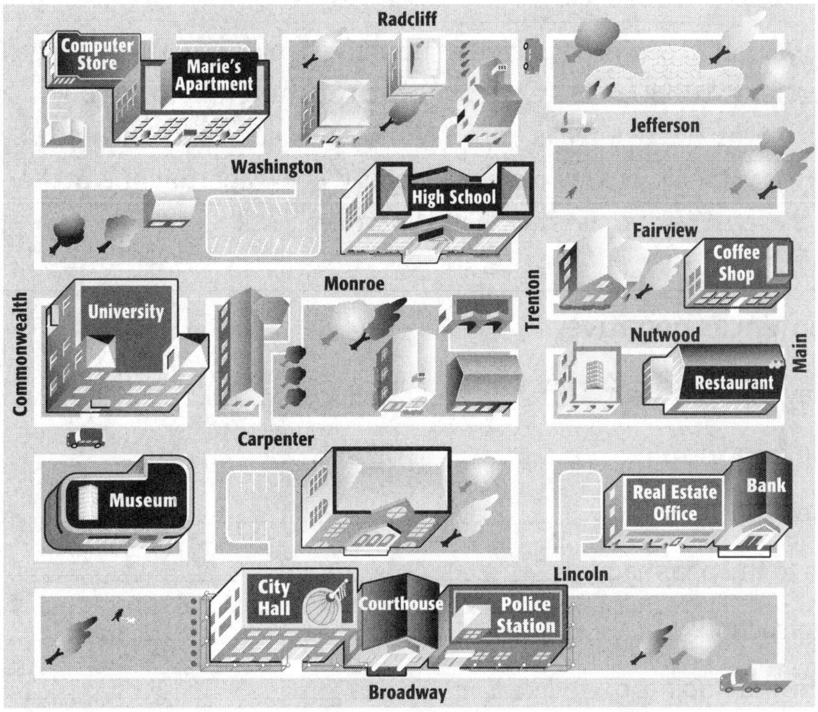

1. Start at the corner of Broadway and Main. Go north on Main Street. Turn left on Nutwood. Turn right on Trenton. What is on the corner of Washington? the high school
2. Start at the corner of Commonwealth and Broadway. Go east on Broadway. Stop on the left. What is before the Courthouse? ____________________
3. Start at the corner of Commonwealth and Radcliff. Go south on Commonwealth. Turn left on Washington. What is on the left before the high school? ____________________

C. Read the chart.

Imperatives			
	(Negative) Verb	Information	Example sentence
~~you~~	**(don't) go**	straight straight ahead	**Go** straight three blocks. **Don't go** straight ahead.
	(don't) turn	left right around	**Turn** left on Nutwood. **Don't turn** right on Nutwood. **Turn** around.
	(don't) stop	on the left on the right	**Stop** on the left. **Don't stop** on the right.

D. Underline the imperatives in the following paragraph. The first one is done for you.

Here are the directions to get to my new apartment from the bank. <u>Go</u> north on Emerson Street. Walk straight ahead for two blocks. There is a pharmacy on the left. Turn left on Michigan Avenue. Go two blocks. At the intersection of Michigan Avenue and Lincoln Street, turn right. Don't turn left; that's the way to my old apartment. My new apartment is at the end of Lincoln Street, on the left. Walk up the stairs. Find apartment 3.

E. Make the affirmative sentences negative.

1. Go to the post office today. *Don't go to the post office today.*
2. Write your address on the form. ______
3. Complete all the customer forms now. ______
4. Walk from the post office to the pharmacy. ______
5. Turn right at the next intersection. ______
6. Stop at the corner of Main and Robinson. ______

F. Make the negative sentences affirmative.

1. Don't send the package economy class. *Send the package economy class.*
2. Don't buy insurance for the package. ______
3. Don't turn left at the corner. ______
4. Don't go west on Broadway. ______

G. Give directions using the map in Exercise B.

1. You are at the corner of Commonwealth and Radcliff. Give directions to the university.

______

______

2. You are at the corner of Main and Jefferson. Give directions to the museum.

______

______

3. You are at the intersection of Trenton and Lincoln. Give directions to the courthouse.

______

______

UNIT 5

LESSON 4 Dear Raquel

GOAL ■ Read a message or letter

A. Read the letter and answer the questions.

Dear Claudia,

How are you? I'm studying English here in Palm City with my good friend Marie. We go to school every day, but Marie also works Monday through Friday at the hospital. Sometimes we meet in the park near her work for lunch. I often walk past the post office on my way to class in the mornings. I hope to receive a letter from you one day.

I'm very happy here, but I miss Antonio. I'm working hard. My English is improving quickly, so I can go home soon. I hope to see you before I leave. Please write.

Your friend,
Raquel

1. Where does Raquel sometimes eat lunch?
   a. at the post office
   b. in the park
   c. at school
2. Why is Raquel going home soon?
   a. Her English is improving quickly.
   b. She is happy.
   c. She wants to see Antonio.
3. What does Raquel often walk past on her way to class?
   a. the post office
   b. Claudia
   c. the hospital
4. Who is Marie?
   a. a friend of Raquel's
   b. a friend of Claudia's
   c. an old friend of Antonio's

B. Who do you write messages to? Check (✓) how often you write messages.

Reason	Often	Sometimes	Rarely	Never
to family				
to friends				
to co-workers (people you work with)				
to teachers or classmates				

C. How do you write messages? Check (✓) how often you write messages.

Reason	Often	Sometimes	Rarely	Never
social media				
e-mails				
text messages				
letters through the mail				

D. Read the charts.

<table>
<tr><th colspan="5">Simple Present</th></tr>
<tr><th>Subject</th><th>Verb</th><th>Subject</th><th>Verb</th><th></th></tr>
<tr><td rowspan="2">I, You, We, They</td><td rowspan="2">eat</td><td>I</td><td>am</td><td rowspan="3">happy
sad
tired</td></tr>
<tr><td>You, We, They</td><td>are</td></tr>
<tr><td>He, She</td><td>eats</td><td>He, She, It</td><td>is</td></tr>
</table>

<table>
<tr><th colspan="4">Present Continuous</th></tr>
<tr><th>Subject</th><th>Be</th><th>Base + ing</th><th>Example sentence</th></tr>
<tr><td>I</td><td>am</td><td>writing</td><td>I am writing this letter in English.</td></tr>
<tr><td>You, We, They</td><td>are</td><td>going</td><td>We are going to the mall.</td></tr>
<tr><td>He, She</td><td>is</td><td>eating</td><td>He is eating at the coffee shop.</td></tr>
<tr><td colspan="4">• Use simple present with always, often, usually, never, sometimes, and every day.
• Use the present continuous with right now, at the moment, and today.</td></tr>
</table>

E. Check (✓) the correct answers.

1. You never ________ to the hardware store. ☐ are going ☑ go
2. Today she ________ in the morning. ☐ is working ☐ works
3. Michel sometimes ________ Marie. ☐ visits ☐ is visiting
4. They always ________ to the museum. ☐ are going ☐ go
5. I ________ in a condominium at the moment. ☐ live ☐ am living

F. Complete each sentence with the correct form of the simple present or the present continuous.

1. I ___am going___ (go) to the dentist today.
2. Today I ________________ (take) the bus.
3. My sister usually ________________ (go) with me.
4. At the moment, we ________________ (wait) at the bus stop on Main Street.
5. The bus always ________________ (stop) at the corner of Main and Washington.

G. Complete the letter for yourself.

Dear ______________,

How are you? I'm fine. At the moment, I ______________ (go) to school in ______________. I ______________ (be) studying English. My school ______________ (be) called ______________ (school name). My class starts at ______________. I always ______________ (work) hard. My teacher ______________ (be) very friendly. Right now, we ______________ (learn) about ______________.

Your friend,

____

UNIT 5

LESSON 5 The city is beautiful

GOAL ■ Write and send a letter

A. Write the letter pieces in the correct sections.

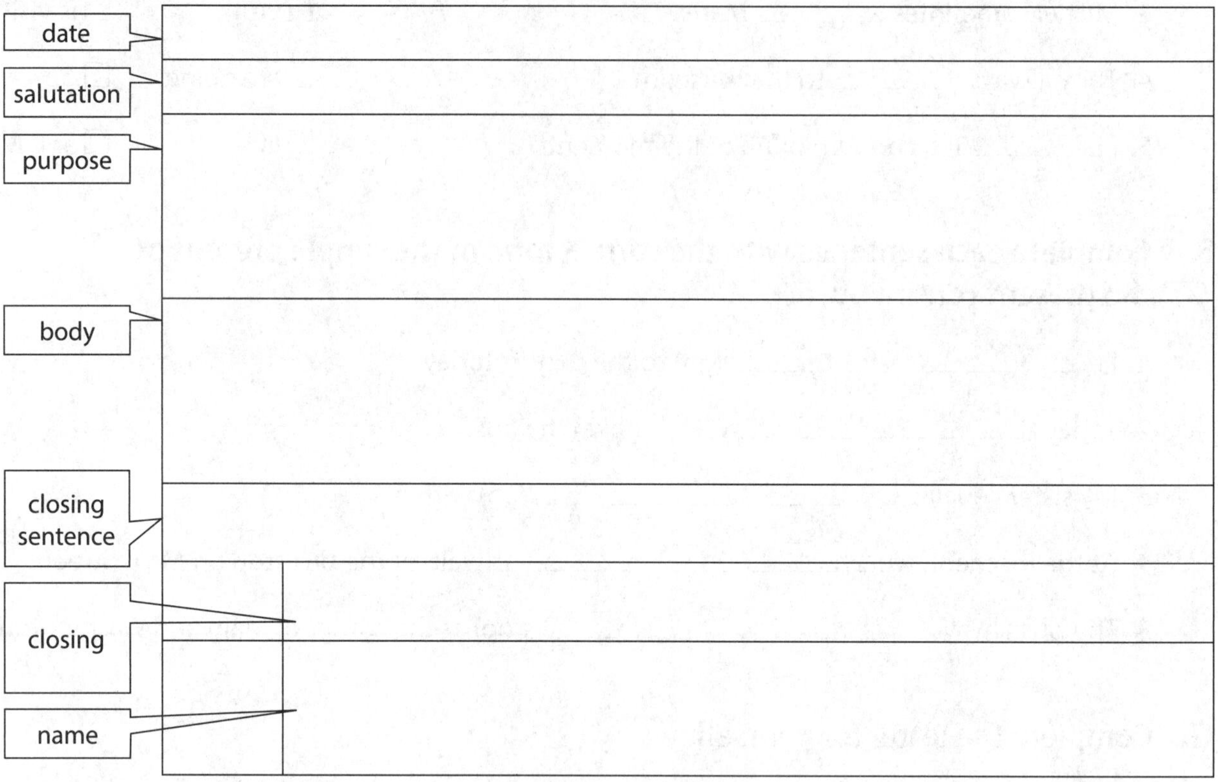

I am writing this letter because we plan to move at the end of next month. I wanted to tell you so you have time to rent the apartment to a new tenant.

Alex Robinson
Alex Robinson (alex.robinson@ma1l.com)
Apartment 302

I am cleaning the apartment right now. There is no problem with the apartment, so I hope we get the deposit back. I have enclosed the rent check of $1,200 for this month. If you have any questions, please e-mail me. Also, let me know if I need to do anything else.

Thank you for all your help.

Dear Mr. Franks,

Sincerely,

January 24th

B. Complete the envelope with the information in the boxes below.

To:

8246 Wilson St.	97701
John Gil	Bend, OR

From:

33010	Miami, FL
~~Jennifer Gault~~	895 Main Place

C. Read the charts.

Simple Past (Regular)		
Subject	**Verb (base + *ed*)**	**Example sentence**
I, You, He, She, It, We, They	talked wanted walked	I **talked** with Marie. She **wanted** a sandwich. We **walked** in the park.

Simple Past (Irregular)		
Subject	**Verb**	**Example sentence**
I, You, He, She, It, We, They	went (go) ate (eat) bought (buy) sent (send)	I **went** to the park. She **ate** at the coffee shop. We **bought** new dresses. They **sent** a letter.

D. Complete the sentences with the simple past.

1. She ___wanted___ (want) a new job.
2. Raquel and Marie ________________ (buy) lunch at Taco Town.
3. You ________________ (go) to school every day.
4. We ________________ (walk) to the post office for the mail.
5. I ________________ (eat) with my friend.
6. She ________________ (talk) to the doctor about her husband.

E. Complete the letter with the simple past form of the verbs in parentheses.

Dear Kenji,

How are you? I'm now living in Palm City. I'm so happy here. I ___went___ to school yesterday for my first day. The teacher __________ (talk) to me about my goals.

After class, I __________ (go) to a restaurant with my new classmates for lunch. We __________ (eat) sushi, and we __________ (talk) about our goals.

I hope to receive a letter from you soon.

Your friend,

Marco

F. Answer the questions with complete sentences. Predict what your classmate did.

1. What did you eat last night for dinner?

   ____

2. What did a classmate eat last night for dinner?

   ____

3. Who did you talk to after class last week?

   ____

4. Who did a classmate talk to after class last week?

   ____

5. Where did you go last week after class?

   ____

6. Where did a classmate go last week after class?

   ____

PRACTICE TEST

A. Look at the map and circle the correct answers.

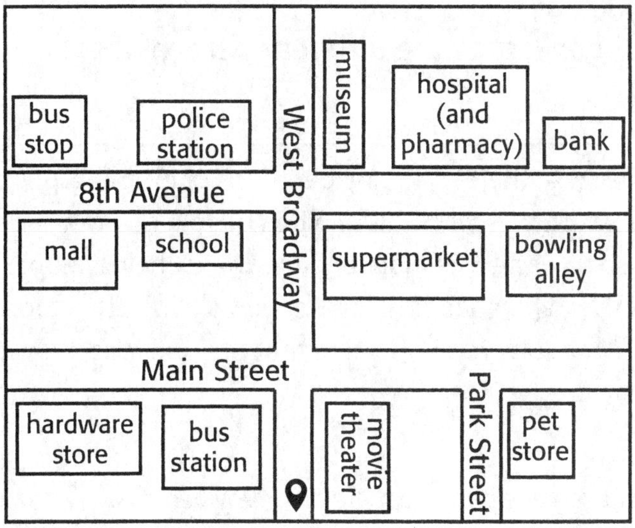

1. The movie theater is on ______________.
   a. Park Street
   b. 8th Street
   c. across from the bus station
   d. the corner of West Broadway and Park Street

2. The bowling alley is ______________ the supermarket.
   a. between
   b. across from
   c. next to
   d. on the corner of

3. The police station is ______________.
   a. opposite the school
   b. next to the mall
   c. on the corner of Main Street
   d. on Park Street

4. Go straight ahead two blocks and turn left. Go to the end of 8th Avenue and stop on the right. Where are you?
   a. the bus stop
   b. the bank
   c. the museum
   d. the mall

5. You need some medicine. Where do you go?
   a. the pharmacy
   b. the bank
   c. the bus station
   d. the police station

6. You are looking for entertainment. Where do you go?
   a. the hardware store
   b. the movie theater
   c. the school
   d. the pet store

UNIT 6

LESSON 1 A healthy life

GOAL ■ Describe healthy practices

A. Read about the benefits of exercise. Then, study the different parts of the paragraph.

Exercise is important for everyone because there are many benefits. For example, people who exercise regularly can control their weight. This is because when people do physical activities, they burn calories. Exercise also gives people more energy. Energy helps people work better and helps them be more active. When people exercise, they sleep better, too. This helps people to think more clearly. For adults, it is important that they exercise every day for 30 minutes or more.

1. **Topic sentence:** *Exercise is important for everyone because there are many benefits.*
2. **Paragraph body:** Examples and details.
3. **Conclusion:** *For adults, it is important that they exercise every day for 30 minutes or more.*

B. Explain each benefit of exercise to complete the examples and details.

1. **Benefit:** control weight ____________________

   Detail: *When people do physical activities, they burn* ____________________.

2. **Benefit:** more ____________________

   Detail: *It helps* ____________________.

3. **Benefit:** ____________________

   Detail: ____________________

C. **Read about the students' habits and rank them. *1* is the student with the healthiest habits.**

Name: Kenji
Sleep: 7 hours
Exercise: 10 minutes
Eat: 2 meals

Name: Gilberto
Sleep: 8 hours
Exercise: 30 minutes
Eat: 3 meals

Name: Lien
Sleep: 9 hours
Exercise: 0 minutes
Eat: 3 meals

1. *Gilberto*
2. ______________________
3. ______________________

D. **Read the chart.**

Verb + Infinitive			
Subject	**Verb**	**Infinitive (*to* + base)**	**Example sentence**
I, You, We, They	want need like	to { sleep, relax, work, drink, eat, exercise }	I **want to sleep** eight hours. You **need to relax** after work. We **like to work** in the morning. They **want to drink** a lot of water. He **likes to eat** a snack in the afternoon. She **likes to exercise** regularly.
He, She	wants needs likes		

E. Circle the correct word or words.

1. Kim (likes to) / likes eat pizza for lunch.
2. Larry and Jean want / want to good food for dinner.
3. We need / need to exercise every day.
4. I like / like to walk in the morning.
5. Kenji likes to / likes pizza for lunch.
6. We work to / work on Saturday.
7. You need / need to drink a lot of water.
8. They relax to / relax after dinner.

F. Complete the sentences.

1. Edgar ____wants to____ (want) work on Saturday.
2. Natalie ________________ (need) exercise more.
3. Karen and Grace ________________ (eat) three meals a day.
4. Kenji ________________ (exercise) for ten minutes a day.
5. Paul and Claudia ________________ (want) shoes for work.
6. Tien and Huong ________________ (drink) water at dinner.
7. Gilberto ________________ (need) sleep more.
8. Cathy ________________ (like) relax at night.

G. Complete the survey.

1. How many hours do you sleep each night?
   a. 2–4 hours b. 5–7 hours c. 8–9 hours d. 10 or more hours
2. How many balanced meals do you eat each day?
   a. 0 meals b. 1 meal c. 2 meals d. 3 meals
3. How many hours do you exercise each week?
   a. 0 hours b. 1–2 hours c. 3–4 hours d. 5 or more hours
4. How many times do you see the doctor for a checkup every year?
   a. 0 times b. 1–2 times c. 3–4 times d. 5 or more times

LESSON 2 What's the matter?

GOAL ■ Identify illnesses

A. Read the e-mail. Underline the parts of the body and write them below.

Send Now | Send Later | Save as Draft | Delete | Add Attachment | Signature

To: ana@ma1l.com

Cc:

Subject: Doctor's Visit

Dear Ana,

I went to the doctor today. He looked into my <u>eyes</u> and said they look good. You know I've been having headaches and trouble seeing. He said he thought it was stress. When I told him about my chest pains, he was a little worried. He said I should take some aspirin, put my feet up, and call him right away when that happens. He said he would do some tests. Sometimes my head hurts so bad that my stomach starts to give me trouble, too.

How are your back and neck? I hope you are feeling better. I know how bad it is to have back problems. Have you talked to the doctor? Write me and tell me how you are doing.

Patricia

_____eyes_____ ______________ ______________ ______________

______________ ______________ ______________

B. Answer the questions about the e-mail in Exercise A.

1. Why does the doctor think Patricia has headaches and trouble seeing?
   - a. He thinks she has a cold.
   - b. He thinks she has the flu.
   - c. He thinks she is stressed.
   - d. He thinks she is having a heart attack.

2. What does the doctor say to do if Patricia feels chest pains?
   - a. take aspirin
   - b. watch TV
   - c. take a test
   - d. exercise

C. Which ailments are most common? Number the ailments *1–8*. *1* is the most common.

______ a backache

______ a cold

______ a headache

______ a runny nose

______ a sore throat

______ a stomachache

______ a toothache

______ the flu

AILMENTS
An ailment is a minor illness.

D. Read the charts.

Adjective	Comparative adjective	Superlative adjective
serious	more serious less serious	the most serious the least serious
common	more common less common	the most common the least common

<table>
<tr><th>Comparatives</th><th>Superlatives</th></tr>
<tr><td>The flu is more serious than a cold.</td><td rowspan="2">Sometimes a toothache is the most serious ailment and a cold is the least serious.</td></tr>
<tr><td>A stomachache is less serious than a toothache.</td></tr>
<tr><td>A headache is more common than the flu.</td><td rowspan="2">Maybe a cold is the most common ailment and a toothache is the least common.</td></tr>
<tr><td>A toothache is less common than a cold.</td></tr>
</table>

E. Use the words to make sentences. Sometimes there can be more than one answer.

1. is / serious / a cold / than / more / a runny nose
   A cold is more serious than a runny nose.
2. the most / a sore throat / serious / is / ailment
   ____
3. common / is / the / than / flu / more / toothache / a
   ____
4. less / serious / a backache / than / a runny nose / is
   ____
5. the / common / most / ailment / is / a headache
   ____

F. Answer the questions about the ailments in Exercise C with complete sentences.

1. What is more serious—the flu or a cold?
   The flu is more serious than a cold.
2. What is more serious—a sore throat, a runny nose, or a cold?
   ____
3. What is more common—a backache or a toothache?
   ____
4. What is less serious—a headache or a cold?
   ____
5. What is less common—a sore throat or a headache?
   ____

G. Write sentences about serious and common ailments.

1. (most serious) ______________________________
2. (most common) ______________________________
3. (least serious) ______________________________
4. (least common) ______________________________

UNIT 6

LESSON 3 Calling for an appointment

GOAL ■ Make a doctor's appointment

A. Read the conversations and complete the agenda.

April 6th				
Name	**Time**	**Problem/Reason for visit**	**Phone**	**New patient?**
1. *Arnold Halley*				*No*
2.				
3.				

Receptionist: Hello, Dr. Rampal's office.

Patient: Yes, I need an appointment.

Receptionist: What's your name?

Patient: It's Arnold Halley.

Receptionist: And your number?

Patient: (777) 543-2396. I have a terrible headache.

Receptionist: I see. Can you come in at 2:00 p.m. today?

Patient: Yes, that sounds fine.

Receptionist: This is Dr. Rampal's office. What can I do for you?

Patient: This is Alexi Zoe.

Receptionist: Oh, Mr. Zoe. You are our new patient, right?

Patient: Yes, how did you know?

Receptionist: Your last doctor called. He gave us your number. That's (777) 932-9988, right?

Patient: Right. I need a checkup.

Receptionist: OK. I will schedule you for 2:30 p.m. today. Is that OK?

Patient: Can you make it 3:00 p.m.?

Receptionist: That will work. See you then.

Receptionist: Hello, Dr. Rampal's office. Can I help you?

Patient: This is Maria Salazar. Can I make an appointment?

Receptionist: Yes, let me confirm your number. Is it still (777) 555-6891?

Patient: No, it's now (777) 555-2349. I think I have an ear infection.

Receptionist: OK. Let's get you in at 4:00 p.m.

Patient: OK.

B. Match the phrases to make sentences.

1. Anya talked
2. She exercised
3. She walked
4. She also smoked

a. in the park every day.
b. cigarettes.
c. to a doctor.
d. three times a week.

C. Write the sentences in Exercise B in a paragraph.

Anya talked to a doctor.

D. Read the charts.

Regular Simple Past	
Subject	**Verb (base + *ed*)**
I, You, He, She, We, They	walked (walk) talked (talk) smoked (smoke) played (play)

Irregular Simple Past	
Subject	**Verb**
I, You, He, She, We, They	had (have) went (go) said (say)

Irregular Simple Past: *Be*		
Subject	***Be***	**Example sentence**
I, He, She	was	I **was** sick.
You, We, They	were	You **were** at the hospital.

E. Circle the correct verb form.

1. Last year, Luc has / (had) some health problems.
2. His wife be / was very nervous.
3. I were / was very healthy last year.
4. I had / having a good exercise plan.
5. You were / was sick last week.
6. You had / having a headache.
7. My wife and I has / had a bad day yesterday.
8. We was / were both very tired.
9. My dog had / have a broken leg last year.
10. The children was / were very sad about it.

F. Complete the sentences with the simple past tense of the verbs.

1. Last week, Alex ____exercised____ (exercise) every day.
2. He also ________________ (play) tennis on Saturday.
3. He ________________ (want) his wife to play tennis, too.
4. On Saturday, she ________________ (visit) the doctor.
5. She ________________ (ask) for medicine to give her more energy.
6. She ________________ (need) more exercise and not medicine.
7. She also ________________ (smoke) a pack of cigarettes a day.
8. She ________________ (talk) to her husband about it.

G. Write the sentences in Exercise F in a paragraph.

Last week, Alex exercised every day.

UNIT 6

LESSON 4 Take two tablets

GOAL Read medicine labels

A. Look at the table and write sentences.

Uses	Take antacid	Use antiseptic cream	Take aspirin	Take cold capsules	Take cough syrup	Take throat lozenges
for burns		✓				
for colds				✓		
for coughs					✓	✓
for cuts and scrapes		✓				
for headaches			✓			
for fevers			✓			
for muscle aches			✓			
for stomachaches	✓					

1. **burns:** Use antiseptic cream for burns.
2. **colds:** ______________________
3. **coughs:** ______________________
4. **cuts and scrapes:** ______________________
5. **headaches:** ______________________
6. **fevers:** ______________________
7. **muscle aches:** ______________________
8. **stomachaches:** ______________________

B. Read the information. Write *U* for *Uses*, *D* for *Directions*, and *W* for *Warnings*.

__D__ Take one or two tablets with water every four hours while symptoms persist.

__U__ For temporary relief of sore throat pain.

_____ Spray four times into throat.

_____ For external use only.

_____ For temporary relief of cold and flu symptoms.

__W__ Do not drive a motor vehicle while taking this medication.

_____ To help prevent infection in minor cuts and scrapes.

_____ Children with the flu or chicken pox should NOT take this medication.

_____ Take two capsules three times a day.

_____ Apply a small amount of the ointment three times a day.

_____ If sore throat pain persists, contact your doctor.

_____ For relief of headache and muscle pain.

C. Read the charts.

Modal: *Should*			
Subject	*Should*	Base verb	Example sentence
I, You, He, She, We, They	should	take talk take swallow	I **should** take two tablets. He **should** talk to the doctor. You **should** take this medicine for a headache. They **should** swallow this tablet with water.

Modal: *Shouldn't*			
Subject	*Should*	Base verb	Example sentence
I, You, He, She, We, They	should not shouldn't	take drink chew	You **shouldn't** take this pill with other medicine. He **shouldn't** drink alcohol with this medicine. She **shouldn't** chew this tablet.

D. Read the problems. Use the instructions to give advice using *should*.

1. I need some aspirin. (go to the drugstore) You should go to the drugstore.
2. We are very tired. (sleep eight hours tonight) ______
3. Ricardo has a cough. (take some cough syrup) ______
4. I broke my arm. (go to the hospital) ______
5. You have a fever. (go to bed) ______
6. Luisa has a headache. (take some aspirin) ______
7. Those men smoke too much. (stop smoking) ______
8. My eyes hurt. (go to the optometrist) ______

E. Complete the sentences with *should* or *shouldn't*.

1. You shouldn't play soccer today. (no)
2. I ______ stop smoking. (yes)
3. Carla ______ eat fatty foods. (no)
4. You ______ take aspirin if you have the chicken pox. (no)
5. The children ______ have a checkup every year. (yes)
6. Ivan ______ take his medicine three times a day. (yes)
7. You ______ make an appointment with the doctor. (yes)
8. They ______ be nervous all the time. (no)
9. I ______ take some cough syrup for my cough. (yes)
10. We ______ drink too much coffee. (no)

F. Write advice for a cold.

1. You should ______.
2. ______
3. You shouldn't ______.
4. ______

UNIT 6

LESSON 5 It's an emergency!

GOAL ■ Identify and describe emergencies

A. Check (✓) the type of emergency.

	Medical	Police	Fire	Not an Emergency
A cat is in a tree.				✓
He accidentally drank poison.				
He coughs every day.				
He hit a tree with my car.				
I am very tired.				
My car is on fire.				
My car was stolen.				
She broke her arm.				
She has a cold.				
She has a sore throat.				
She has a stomachache.				
She is having a heart attack.				
The house is on fire.				
The man is not breathing.				
There is a strange man in my house.				
There is no food in the house.				
They have the flu.				

B. Read the paragraph and answer the questions.

911 Operators and Emergencies

911 is a very important number. Sometimes more calls come to the operators than they can answer. 911 operators have a difficult job. They have to decide which calls are the most important. People are often excited or nervous when they call. The operator should stay calm. People calling should explain the problem and give all the important information, including their name and address. The 911 operator should be patient. The operator's job is to call the correct emergency service. Sometimes people call about things that are not emergencies. It is important to call 911 ONLY in the case of an emergency.

1. What should the 911 operator do in case of an emergency?
   a. go home early
   b. call the correct emergency service
   c. talk to the supervisor

2. What information should the caller give?
   a. his or her name and address
   b. his or her driver's license number
   c. the emergency service number

C. Read the chart.

Simple Past: Irregular Verbs		
Key verbs with a spelling change in the simple past tense		
break — broke	find — found	sit — sat
buy — bought	get — got	sleep — slept
come — came	go — went	take — took
do — did	pay — paid	understand — understood
drink — drank	read — read*	wake — woke
drive — drove	say — said**	wear — wore
eat — ate	see — saw	write — wrote
*the past tense sounds like *red*	***said* rhymes with *red*	
Key verbs with no change in the simple past tense		
hurt — hurt	put — put	cost — cost

D. Complete each sentence with the simple past tense of the verb in parentheses.

1. I ___broke___ (break) my arm last week.
2. You ________ (wake) up at 7:00 a.m.
3. You ________ (go) to the doctor at noon.
4. Your parents ________ (buy) you some aspirin.
5. They ________ (come) to visit you.
6. Teresa ________ (do) some exercises.
7. She ________ (eat) a healthy breakfast.
8. Dan ________ (sleep) eight hours last night.
9. He ________ (take) some vitamins.
10. I ________ (get) sick yesterday.
11. My sister ________ (say) she was sick, too.
12. We ________ (drink) a lot of orange juice.

E. Rewrite each sentence in the simple past tense.

1. I wake up at 6:00 a.m. ___I woke up at 6:00 a.m.___
2. You drive me to the doctor at noon. ________
3. The doctor says to take some medicine. ________
4. I get the medicine from the doctor. ________
5. You read the directions. ________
6. I take two teaspoons of the syrup. ________
7. I sleep for ten hours. ________
8. We eat a good breakfast. ________
9. My friends come to see me. ________
10. They buy me some flowers. ________

F. On a separate piece of paper, write a conversation about an emergency between a 911 operator and a caller.

PRACTICE TEST

A. Read and circle the correct answers.

A doctor's checkup once a year is a very good idea. The doctor will give you a physical and check your heart, your lungs, your ears, and eyes. If you think you have a medical problem, this is the time to talk to the doctor. For some problems, the doctor will probably ask you to get a blood test. Most doctors want to see adults once a year, but sometimes if you have a medical problem and need to take medicine, you should visit twice a year or more. Checkups are important because the doctor checks your health and can find problems early before they are serious.

1. How often should adults get a checkup if they take medicine regularly?
   a. two or more times a year
   b. for medical problems
   c. every month
   d. a physical
2. Who takes medicine prescribed by the doctor?
   a. all people who visit the doctor
   b. for your heart
   c. people with medical problems
   d. people with no medical problems
3. Why is it good to have a checkup?
   a. for blood tests
   b. to give you medicine
   c. so doctors can find health problems early
   d. a physical

B. Read the medicine label and circle the correct answers.

1. Why do you take this medicine?
   a. two teaspoons
   b. not for children under 12
   c. for coughs
   d. four hours
2. How often can you take the medicine?
   a. two teaspoons
   b. not for children under 12
   c. for cough
   d. every four hours
3. Who should take the medicine?
   a. people over 12
   b. two teaspoons
   c. for coughs
   d. every four hours
4. How much cough syrup should you take each time?
   a. two teaspoons
   b. one throat lozenge
   c. every four hours
   d. every three hours

Medicine Label

Uses: for temporary relief of coughs due to cold or flu.

Directions: take two teaspoons every four hours as needed.

Warning: do not give to children under 12.

UNIT 7

LESSON 1 A good student and employee

GOAL ■ Evaluate learning and work skills

A. Evaluate your study skills. Take a survey.

Study Habits Questionnaire

1. How often do you come to class?
   - ☐ a. most of the time ☐ b. sometimes ☐ c. less than 50%
2. Do you come to class on time?
   - ☐ a. most of the time ☐ b. sometimes ☐ c. less than 50%
3. How much do you study at home each week?
   - ☐ a. more than 10 hours ☐ b. 5–10 hours ☐ c. less than 5 hours
4. Do you speak English in class and participate?
   - ☐ a. most of the time ☐ b. sometimes ☐ c. less than 50%
5. Do you teach and help other students in class?
   - ☐ a. a lot ☐ b. a little ☐ c. never
6. Do you listen to the radio in English?
   - ☐ a. a lot ☐ b. a little ☐ c. never
7. Do you watch TV in English?
   - ☐ a. a lot ☐ b. a little ☐ c. never
8. Do you ask the teacher or other students questions when you don't understand?
   - ☐ a. a lot ☐ b. a little ☐ c. never

How many *a* answers, *b* answers, and *c* answers do you have?		
# of ***a*** answers _____	# of ***b*** answers _____	# of ***c*** answers _____

Do the math below.

of ***a*** answers x 3 = _____
of ***b*** answers x 2 = _____
of ***c*** answers x 1 = _____
Total = _____

Score: **20–24**	Super – You have great study habits!
Score: **16–19**	Good – You can improve some study habits.
Score: **Under 16**	– You need to change your study habits.

B. Read the conversation and mark the evaluation with *S, G,* or *NI*.

EVALUATION							
Date: August 10th		Name: Vincent Nunez		Supervisor: Betty Moore			
1. Comes to work on time	S	G	NI	4. Works well with a team	S	G	NI
2. Follows instructions	S	G	NI	5. Understands the job	S	G	NI
3. Helps others	S	G	NI	6. Has a positive attitude	S	G	NI
S=Superior G=Good NI=Needs Improvement				Betty Moore			

Supervisor: Vincent, I want to go over your evaluation.

Vincent: OK, I try to do a good job.

Supervisor: Yes, I see that every day. I have given you a *superior* for coming to work on time and understanding the job. I have also marked *good* for attitude.

Vincent: Why do I not have a *superior* for attitude?

Supervisor: . . . because you don't help other employees or want to work in a team. See, both of these areas are *needs improvement*.

Vincent: Is working in a team important for my job?

Supervisor: Absolutely! It's important for every job.

Vincent: I will improve. I'll begin today to work with the other employees.

Supervisor: I was sure you would. That is why I gave you a *superior* for following instructions.

C. Read the charts.

Future: *Will* (Affirmative)			
Subject	***Will***	**Base verb**	**Example sentence**
I, You, He, She, We, They	will	come listen help work have	I **will** come to class on time. You **will** listen carefully and follow instructions. They **will** help other students. We **will** work hard. He **will** have a positive attitude.

Future: *Will* (Negative)			
Subject	***Will***	**Base verb**	**Example sentence**
I, You, He, She, We, They	will not (won't)	come leave forget	I **won't** come to class late. You **won't** leave class early. He **won't** forget his homework.

D. Circle the correct future verb form.

1. Vincent (will work) / will working on a team in the future.
2. Raquel is listen / will listen to the teacher next week.
3. Marie and Raquel is coming / will come to class on time tomorrow.
4. I will follow / will following instructions at work in the future.
5. We will leave / are leave class at 6:00 p.m. tomorrow.
6. You are having / will have a better attitude after you eat.
7. She wills need / will need assistance from another worker.
8. Jean won't / wills not smoke at work.
9. Lien and Duong are having / will have homework.
10. Tuba will leaves / will leave for Texas in the morning.

E. Rewrite the statements in the future affirmative and negative.

1. Lydia comes to work on time.
   a. Lydia will come to work on time.
   b. Lydia won't come to work on time.
2. The Nguyen brothers follow instructions well.
   a. __________
   b. __________
3. I help others at every opportunity.
   a. __________
   b. __________
4. We work well in a team.
   a. __________
   b. __________

F. Check (✓) what you will do in the future.

☐ study English ☐ work tomorrow ☐ do my homework
☐ listen in class ☐ come to school on time ☐ smoke in class

G. Write one negative and one affirmative sentence with information from Exercise F.

1. __________
2. __________

UNIT 7

LESSON 2 What can you do?

GOAL ■ Identify jobs and job skills

A. Match the job skills to the job titles.

	Job title	Job skills
f	accountant	a. cleans teeth and takes care of dental issues
	chef	b. creates meals for a restaurant
	counselor	c. fixes problems with pipes in a home
	dentist	d. gives advice and helps people
	firefighter	e. helps people make decisions about purchases
	lawyer	f. manages money for a company
	plumber	g. puts out fires and saves lives
	sales representative	h. represents people with law issues
	administrative assistant	i. serves food in a restaurant
	server	j. schedules meetings and helps in an office

B. Write sentences about the information in Exercise A.

1. An accountant is someone who manages money for a company.
2. A chef is someone who ________________.
3. A counselor is someone who ________________.
4. A dentist ________________.
5. A firefighter ________________.
6. ________________
7. ________________
8. ________________
9. ________________
10. ________________

C. Make a list of ten things Alana can do with the information from her job application.

Name: Alana Kim

SKILLS

Languages: German

Skills: use computer programs, schedule meetings, use office equipment, send memos

JOB HISTORY

Position	Company	Duties
Office Manager	Barcelona Tile	manage paperwork, write newsletters, supervise three employees
Administrative Assistant	Jocelyn's Jewelry Emporium	schedule meetings, answer phones, send memos, speak to customers
File Clerk	Jocelyn's Jewelry Emporium	send memos, file papers

1. *use office equipment*
2. *supervise employees*
3. ______
4. ______
5. ______
6. ______
7. ______
8. ______
9. ______
10. ______

D. Read the chart.

Modal: *Can* (Ability)				
	Subject	***Can***	**Base verb**	**Example sentence**
Affirmative	I	**can**	send	I **can** send memos.
	He, She, It	**can**	use	He/She **can** use a computer.
	We	**can**	fix	We **can** fix things around the house.
Negative	You	**cannot**	speak	You **cannot** speak Spanish.
	They	**can't**	turn	They **can't** turn on the copier.
• The negative of *can* is *cannot*. The contraction is *can't*.				

E. Write what these people *can* and *can't* do.

1. Kenji ___can___ use a computer. (yes)
2. Marie __________ speak Japanese. (no)
3. Anya and Ivan __________ send e-mails. (yes)
4. You __________ put the paper in the printer. (no)
5. We __________ work well together. (yes)
6. I __________ turn on the fax machine. (no)
7. They __________ understand Chinese. (yes)
8. We __________ drive a car. (yes)
9. Sam __________ speak English well. (no)
10. Gilberto __________ prepare food. (yes)
11. I __________ cook well. (no)
12. You __________ teach English. (yes)

F. Use the words to write about what people *can* and *cannot* do.

1. speak / cannot / Russian / I ___I cannot speak Russian.___
2. Sara / the piano / can't / play __________
3. draw / well / cannot / we __________
4. can / the house / things / around / Ivan / fix __________
5. the computer / Dalva / use / can __________
6. a truck / you / drive / can't __________
7. the children / swim / can __________
8. Spanish / teach / cannot / I __________
9. cook / food / Mexican / Mario / can __________
10. can't / Chinese / we / understand __________

G. Check (✓) what you can do.

- ☐ send e-mails
- ☐ answer phones
- ☐ do homework
- ☐ listen in class
- ☐ take messages
- ☐ use office equipment

H. Write sentences about what you *can* and *can't* do using the information from Exercise G.

1. (can) __________
2. (can) __________
3. (can't) __________
4. (can't) __________

LESSON 3 Job hunting

GOAL ■ Apply for a job

A. Read the job advertisement and complete the table.

Experienced Carpenters Wanted

Silverton Chair Manufacturing is looking for experienced carpenters and woodworkers to build quality chairs and tables in our factory on Rosewood Avenue in Rolling Heights, North Carolina. Our business is 35 years old. We have 220 employees throughout the United States. Our wages are very good and start at $14 an hour. We also offer good benefits including 12 sick days and a two-week vacation every year. These positions are full-time. We will only interview applicants with five years or more experience in woodworking. English is required because your duties may include speaking to clients and management. Complete the application online. We will not accept applications after February 22nd. If you have questions, please contact our offices at **(828) 555-3765** and ask for Sergio. You may also send e-mail to **Sergio_Sotelo@ma1l.com.**

Application

Company name	
Company location	
Contact name	
Contact number	
Contact e-mail	
Position available	
Years of experience required	
Full-time or part-time	
Pay	
Two benefits	
Closing date	

B. **Read the classified ads and complete the table.**

DRIVER NEEDED

1 yr. exp, f/t or p/t, gd bnfts, we will train, appl avail. $12/hr. Call 555-7467 M–F, 8–6. **Requirements:** speak English, drive a truck.

Hairstylist

Must know all styles, $15/hr, p/t, 3 yrs. exp req., app. in person. Call for appt. 555-3456. **Requirements:** work on weekends, use a cash register.

ASSEMBLY WORKER

f/t, no exp nec., gd benefits, opp. for advancement, $7.00 to start. Call 555-3456. **Requirements:** speak English, work at night.

Secretary

Exp. nec., p/t only, gd pay and bnfts, vacation and travel, $18/hr. Call 555-9845. **Requirements:** speak Spanish and English, schedule meetings.

Position	Experience	F/T or P/T	Pay
Driver	1 yr.		
Assembly worker			
Hairstylist			
Secretary			

C. **Read the chart.**

Questions with *May* and *Can*			
Can	Subject	Base verb	Example question and answer
can	I, you, he, she, it, we, they	send drive understand work cook clean talk	**Can** you send memos? Yes, I can. **Can** they drive a car? No, they can't. **Can** she understand English? Yes, she can. **Can** I work on Saturdays? Yes, you can. **Can** he cook breakfast? No, he can't. **Can** we clean on the weekend? Yes, you can. **Can** you talk to customers? No, you can't.

D. Write *yes/no* questions to ask what people can do.

1. Anya and Ivan / work on Saturday Can Anya and Ivan work on Saturday?
2. Diem / drive a car ______
3. I / file those letters ______
4. you / send me a resume ______
5. we / talk about the job ______
6. Don / give me his application ______

E. List the requirements for the jobs in the classified ads in Exercise B.

Driver	Assembly worker	Hairstylist	Secretary
speak English			

F. Write interview questions with information from the table in Exercise E.

1. **Driver**

   (Mario) Can Mario speak English?

   (You) ______
2. **Assembly worker**

   (Anya) ______

   (Peter and Jane) ______
3. **Hairstylist**

   (You) ______

   (Kevin) ______
4. **Secretary**

   (You) ______

   (Pilar) ______

UNIT 7

LESSON 4 Job interviews

GOAL ■ Interview for a job

A. Look at the job application and answer the questions in complete sentences.

JOB APPLICATION

PERSONAL INFORMATION **POSITION** – *Nurse*

Name: *Nguyen* (last) *Oahn* (first) (mi) **Phone:** *(444) 654-3811*

Present Address: *77 W. Main St.*

City: *Hampton* **State:** *NY* **Zip:** *10001*

Present Address: *77 W. Main St.*

Special Skills: ______

Languages: *English / Vietnamese*

Computer Skills ______

Employer	Position	Duties	Dates		Reason for leaving
			from	to	
Mercy Hospital	*Head Nurse*	*manage nurses*	*07-15-2009*	*Present*	*Relocating*
Mercy Hospital	*Nurse*	*helped doctors*	*05-2002*	*07-2009*	*New position*
Hart Medical Center	*Nurse's Assistant*	*worked with nurses*	*06-2001*	*05-2002*	*Completed training*
Hart Medical Center	*Receptionist*	*managed patient appointments*	*02-2000*	*06-2001*	*Promotion*

1. What was Oahn's position in July 2001? *She was a nurse's assistant.*
2. What was Oahn's position in 2005? ______
3. What was Oahn's position in 2010? ______
4. What were Oahn's duties in April 2001? ______
5. What were Oahn's duties in 2005? ______
6. What were Oahn's duties in 2010? ______

B. Look at the job application in Exercise A again. Complete two sentences for each job.

EXAMPLE: In 2000, *Oahn was a receptionist*. *She managed patient appointments*.

1. In 2002, ______. ______.
2. In 2007, ______. ______.

C. **Read Hakim's employment history and complete the timeline.**

Employment History *(Please list most recent position first.)*

Employer	Position	Dates from	Dates to	Reason for leaving
Right Value Hotel	3. Hotel manager	02-2015	10-2015	I moved
Right Value Hotel	2. Supervisor	05-2010	07-2014	promotion
Right Value Hotel	1. Housekeeper	10-2009	05-2010	promotion

2009	2010	2011	2012	2013	2014	2015

3.

2.

1. housekeeper

D. **Answer the questions about Hakim's employment history in Exercise C.**

1. How long did he work for Right Value Hotel? ___6___ (years / months)
2. How long did he work as a housekeeper? __________ (years / months)
3. How long did he work as a supervisor? __________ (years / months)
4. How long did he work as a manager? __________ (months)

E. **Read the chart.**

Simple Past	
Negative forms of regular and irregular verbs (except *be*)	
I **didn't work** in the evenings.	We **didn't have** a paid vacation.
Dalva **didn't know** how to use a computer.	You **didn't turn off** the computer.
• For all forms of regular and irregular verbs (except *be*), use *did not* (*didn't*) + base.	
Negative forms of *be*	
I **wasn't** at work today. He/She/It **wasn't** friendly.	We **weren't** happy. You **weren't** in the hospital. They **weren't** at the front desk.
• For the verb *be*, use *was not* (*wasn't*) and *were not* (*weren't*).	

F. Check (✓) the correct negative form to complete each sentence.

1. They ____________ the phone. ☐ didn't answered ☑ didn't answer
2. Last year, Marie ____________ health insurance. ☐ didn't have ☐ doesn't have
3. The resumes ____________ on my desk. ☐ weren't ☐ wasn't
4. Geraldo ____________ as a gardener. ☐ not work ☐ didn't work
5. Marie ____________ French at her old job. ☐ didn't speak ☐ didn't spoke
6. You ____________ about my new job. ☐ didn't ask ☐ didn't asked

G. Complete each sentence with the negative form of the underlined verb.

1. Dalva <u>worked</u> at a hotel. She ___didn't work___ at a hospital.
2. I <u>send</u> memos all day. I ____________ e-mails.
3. I <u>was</u> available for work on Saturday. I ____________ available for work on Sunday.
4. You <u>were</u> interested in a full-time job. You ____________ interested in a part-time job.
5. You <u>knew</u> how to use the fax machine. You ____________ how to use the shredder.
6. We <u>were</u> at the copier. We ____________ at the printer.

H. Rewrite the sentences about Exercise D in the negative.

1. Hakim was a hairstylist from 2009 to 2011.

   Hakim wasn't a hairstylist from 2009 to 2011.

2. He managed the hotel for three years.

   ____

3. He answered the phones in the office in 2012.

   ____

4. Hakim and the other housekeepers worked for free.

   ____

UNIT 7

LESSON 5 How does it work?

GOAL ■ Follow instructions in an office

A. Read the article. Then, match the definitions with the words and phrases.

Following Directions

Following directions in the workplace is very important. Employers like employees who follow directions and do what they are asked to do when they are asked to do it. Some employees try to look like they are working, but really don't work hard. Sometimes they keep their jobs for a while because it is difficult and expensive to change employees a lot.

Employees should listen carefully. It is a good idea for them to write information down so they don't forget. It is also good to do the job well. Employees should not cut corners. They should do the job the way the employers want. Employees should not waste time. They should start the job right away and they should continue until it is complete.

employers	appear
employees	continue to have
look like	use time badly
keep	workers
cut corners	take shortcuts; not do a complete job
waste time	company; boss or manager

B. Write the words under the pictures.

choose close connect press/enter record turn off turn on open

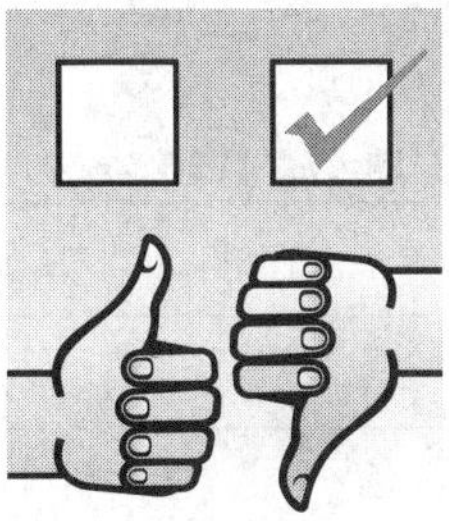

C. Read the chart.

Imperatives	
Affirmative imperative	**Negative imperative**
Write your name on the application.	**Don't write** your age.
Press the green button.	**Don't press** the red button.
Be helpful at work.	**Don't be** late for work.

- The imperative uses the base form of the verb.
- The subject is **you**, but it is not included.
- The negative imperative is *do not* + base form. The contraction is *don't*.
- Imperatives give warnings, directions, or suggestions.
- Use an exclamation mark (!) if the feeling is very strong.

D. Circle the correct imperative sentence.

1. Turn on the copier. / You can turn on the copier. / Turns on the copier.
2. Doesn't connect the printer. / Don't connect the printer. / Connecting the printer.
3. Enters the information. / Enter the information. / enter the information.
4. Records a message. / Recording a message. / Record a message.
5. Choose the answer. / Chooses the answer. / Is choosing an answer.
6. Doesn't close the lid. / Are not close the lid. / Don't close the lid.
7. Open the container. / Opens the container. / You can open the container.
8. Turning off the machine. / Don't off the machine. / Turn off the machine.

E. Make each sentence negative using the words given.

1. Record the new message. (old message) Don't record the old message.
2. Put the paper in the top. (bottom) ____________________
3. Turn off the shredder. (printer) ____________________
4. Press the stop button. (start button) ____________________
5. Enter a number. (name) ____________________
6. Wait for an answer. (beep) ____________________
7. Connect the printer to the computer. (fax) ____________________
8. Place the paper in the top slot. (middle slot) ____________________
9. Keep the printer near the copier. (phone) ____________________
10. Turn off the copier at night. (in the morning) ____________________

F. Write directions for using a microwave oven.

Plug in the microwave.

____

____

____

____

____

PRACTICE TEST

A. Read the job application and circle the correct answers.

JOB APPLICATION

PERSONAL INFORMATION

Name: Arthur Frank Position: Nurse Phone: (731)555-9835

EMPLOYMENT HISTORY *(Please list most recent positions first.)*

Employer	Position	Dates from	Dates to	Reason for leaving
Speedy Tune-Up	Manager	10-2015	Present	Want new experience
Speedy Tune-Up	Mechanic	03-2008	10-2015	New position
Ned's Auto Shop	Mechanic	10-2007	03-2008	New position / Better pay

1. What was Arthur Frank's last job?
   a. manager b. nurse c. mechanic d. Ned's Auto Shop
2. What job is Arthur applying for?
   a. manager b. nurse c. mechanic d. Ned's Auto Shop
3. Why did Arthur Frank leave his job in March, 2008?
   a. new position and better pay b. for a new experience
   c. mechanic d. Speedy Tune-Up

B. Read the evaluation form and circle the correct answers.

1. Why did Fernando get "needs improvement" for punctuality?
   a. He was late.
   b. eight hours
   c. He got a superior.
   d. He talked to customers.
2. What position does Fernando have?
   a. Paul's Radio
   b. Leticia Garcia
   c. sales clerk
   d. supervisor
3. Why was Fernando late?
   a. car trouble
   b. family issues
   c. good knowledge
   d. needs improvement

EVALUATION FORM

DATE: May 4th
COMPANY: Paul's Radio and CD
NAME: Fernando Gaspar
POSITION: Sales Clerk
SUPERVISOR: Leticia Garcia

Punctuality:
Superior Good Needs improvement (circled)

Appearance (professional dress and grooming):
Superior (circled) Good Needs improvement

Communication Skills:
Superior Good (circled) Needs improvement

Product Knowledge:
Superior Good (circled) Needs improvement

Fernando is a good employee. I worked with him for eight hours today. He talked with the customers well. He was ten minutes late to work. This is a problem. He said he had a problem with his car. Fernando is a good salesperson and he has very good knowledge of the product.

SIGNED: Leticia Garcia

UNIT 8

LESSON 1 What is success?

GOAL ■ Identify goals

A. Read the goals and put them in the correct columns.

become a U.S. citizen	get married	take computer classes
~~buy a house~~	lose 10 pounds	have children
get a promotion at work	go to a trade school	work part-time
learn a new skill at work	move	get a high school diploma
get a raise (more money)	go to college	help children in school
learn English	spend more time with my family	work full-time
exercise every day		

Personal and family	Vocational (work)	Academic (educational)
buy a house		

B. Add some of your own personal goals to the table in Exercise A.

C. Read about Anastasia and the things she wants or needs to do. Then, complete the table.

My name's Anastasia and I'm married. At the moment I'm a homemaker, but one day I want to get a high school diploma. I'm not sure what I want to do right now, so I need to think about my career. My husband and I have one child, but one day I want to have more children. My daughter is in first grade and sometimes needs help with her homework. I want to help at her school, but first I need to improve my English because I don't speak very much. We live in a two-bedroom apartment close to her school and my husband's work, but one day I want to buy a house for my family.

Wants to do	Needs to do
have more children	

D. Read the charts.

Express Future Plans: *Want to, Hope to, Plan to*			
Subject	Verb	Infinitive (*to* + base)	
I, You, We, They	**hope, want, plan**	to	**study** English **graduate** from college **get** married **be** a doctor
He, She	**hopes, wants, plans**		

Express Future Plans: *Be going to*			
Subject	*Be going to*	Base verb	Information
I	**am going to**	get	a high school diploma
You, We, They	**are going to**	participate	in my child's school
He, She	**is going to**	buy	a house

want to	*hope to*	*plan to*	*be going to*
less definite →			→ more definite

E. Complete the sentences by using the verbs and forming infinitives.

1. I want to get (want / get) a better job.
2. Marie ______ (be going / study) medicine.
3. We ______ (hope / graduate) from the university.
4. Mario ______ (plan / learn) English at school.
5. Miguel and Anita ______ (be going / become) citizens.
6. You ______ (want / return) to your country.
7. My sister ______ (be going / get) married.
8. I ______ (plan / buy) a house and a car.
9. Many students ______ (be going / have) good careers.
10. We ______ (hope / be) successful.

F. Write the sentences from definite to less definite.

I hope to learn English.	I want to study music.
~~I am going to get a diploma.~~	I plan to be a teacher.

definite I am going to get a diploma.

______

______

less definite ______

G. Complete the sentences about you.

1. I want to ______.
2. I hope to ______.
3. I plan to ______.
4. I am going to ______.

UNIT 8

LESSON 2 Education in the United States

GOAL ■ Set academic goals

A. Study the information and create a bar graph.

1. 17% no high school diploma
2. 34% only a high school diploma
3. 8% AA degree
4. 17% some college but no degree
5. 16% bachelor's degree
6. 8% higher than a Bachelor's degree

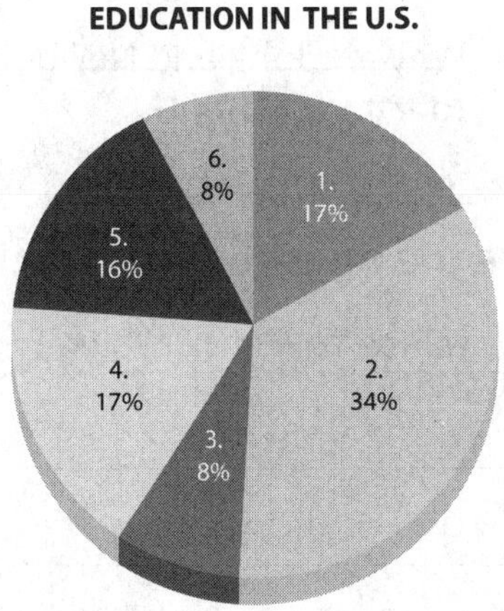

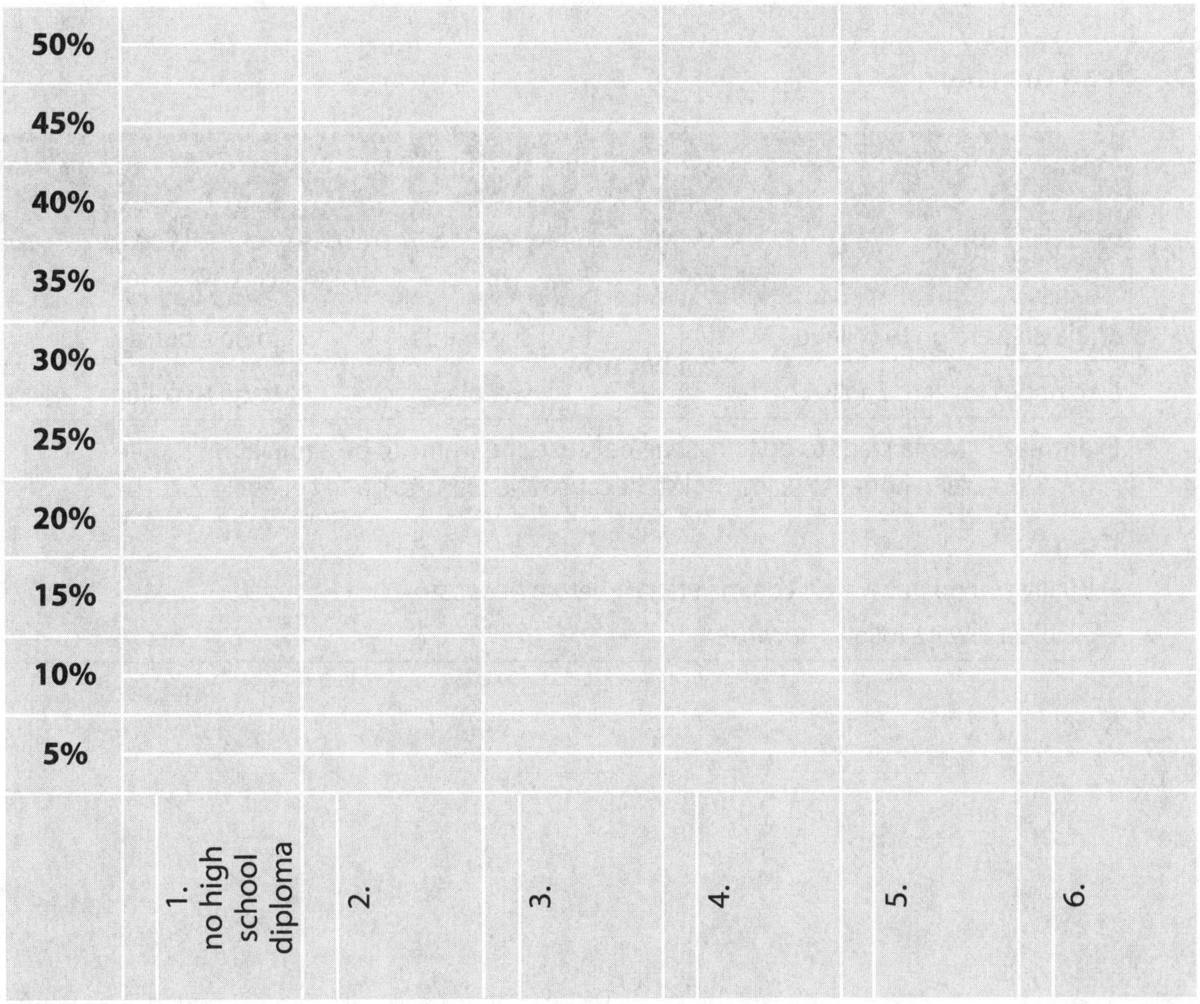

B. Match each question with the reason. Write the correct letter next to each question.

__b__ 1. Why does Maria want to go to college?

_____ 2. Why is Arthur learning English?

_____ 3. Why is Chau happy today?

_____ 4. Why are John and Neil going to a trade school?

a. He graduated from college.

b. She wants to study nursing.

c. They plan to be mechanics.

d. He needs it to speak to his boss.

C. Rewrite the questions in Exercise B as statements.

1. Maria wants to go to college.

2. ______________________________

3. ______________________________

4. ______________________________

D. Read the chart.

Because and Adverbial Clauses			
Reason			
Statement	*Because*	Subject + verb	Information
Maria plans to go to college	**because**	she wants	to be a nurse
Lien hopes to learn English better		she plans	to go to college
Examples: Maria plans to go to college **because** she wants to be a nurse. Lien hopes to learn English **because** she plans to go to college.			
Usage: • Usually you do not write a comma after or before *because*. • A subject always follows *because*.			

E. Combine each sentence with a reason from the box using *because*.

She needs help with the homework.	~~He wants to get a better job.~~
You want to learn quickly.	I want to prepare for the test.
She wants to be a doctor.	They hope to be teachers.

1. John is studying English.

   John is studying English because he wants to get a better job.

2. Karen talks to the teacher.

   ____

3. Annabel plans to go to medical school.

   ____

4. Gilberto and Mario are learning math.

   ____

5. I am going to study all week.

   ____

6. You listen carefully.

   ____

F. Use exercises B and C to write sentences with *because*.

1. Maria wants to go to college because she wants to study nursing.
2. ______________________________
3. ______________________________
4. ______________________________

G. Complete the sentences about your goals.

1. I am studying English because ______________________________.
2. I hope to ______________________ because ______________________.
3. I plan to ______________________ because ______________________.
4. I am going to ______________________ because ______________________.

UNIT 8

LESSON 3 Workplace goals

GOAL ■ Set work goals

A. Read about Gabriel's vocational goals. Underline all instances of *want to, hope to, plan to,* and *be going to.*

1 My name is Gabriel. I have many goals. First of all, I love to cook. At the moment, I'm a cook at my father's restaurant. His restaurant is called Augustine's. I plan to go to cooking school. When I'm finished, I hope to make some new dishes at the restaurant. I want to make dishes from all over the world.

2 I plan to save some money. After I save some money, I am going to buy my own restaurant. I will need some help to start, so I hope to find a business partner to help me. I love to cook, and I think I can be very successful. I hope to serve international food at my restaurant.

3 If I'm successful, I'm going to open another restaurant. After we have two restaurants, we will open more. Of course, we are going to need more partners to help. I think good managers are very important, too. Every restaurant is going to have excellent managers. I am excited to start my plan!

B. Match the paragraph numbers to the topics.

Paragraph 1	More restaurants
Paragraph 2	Father's restaurant
Paragraph 3	His own restaurant

C. Read the timeline and write Gabriel's plans. Use the verbs below to help you.

2016	2018	2019	2021	2023	2025
work in my father's restaurant go to cooking school	cook new foods in my father's restaurant save money	buy a restaurant and serve international food	find a business partner start a second restaurant	find another business partner start another restaurant	hire managers for all restaurants

Remember:

want to	*hope to*	*plan to*	*be going to*
less definite →			more definite

1. Gabriel is going to work in his father's restaurant in 2016.
2. ______________________________
3. ______________________________
4. ______________________________
5. ______________________________
6. ______________________________
7. ______________________________
8. ______________________________
9. ______________________________
10. ______________________________

D. Read the chart.

Future: *Will*			
Subject	***Will***	**Base verb**	**Information**
I, You, He, She, It, We, They	will	go	to school for two more years
		study	English this year
		be	happy

want to	*hope to*	*plan to*	*be going to*	*will*
less definite →				very definite

E. Rewrite the sentences using *will* to express future.

1. Ahmed goes to a trade school. Ahmed will go to a trade school.
2. I have a new job. ______
3. Lien is a counselor. ______
4. I need a part-time job. ______
5. We graduate in the spring. ______
6. Mario owns an auto repair business. ______
7. Martina and Ana study accounting. ______
8. We save money. ______
9. You work in a library. ______
10. I apply for a library card. ______

F. Write the correct verb to express the future.

1. Gabriel hopes to have (hope / have) three restaurants by 2023.
2. Gabriel and Francisco ______ (plan / work) together.
3. We ______ (will / study) cooking in 2016.
4. Gabriel ______ (will / go) to cooking school.
5. Gabriel and Angela ______ (hope / get) married in 2019.
6. I ______ (be going / see) Gabriel soon.

G. Make your own timeline and tell a partner about your plans for the future.

2016	2018	2020
2022	**2024**	**2026**

UNIT 8

LESSON 4 Lifelong learning

GOAL ■ Find ways to learn

A. Read about Amad's goals and answer the questions.

Amad is a good student and he is happy with his job, but he doesn't want to do the same thing forever. He has some problems. First, he and his wife want to have a big family, but he doesn't make enough money. He needs to find another job. Right now, he works part-time and he needs to work full-time. He is very good with computers, but he doesn't speak English, so it is difficult to get a job.

Amad also has a goal to get a college degree someday. He is thinking about it, but he doesn't know exactly what to do. A degree will help him find a better job in the future. He needs to find a college to go to. He doesn't know what to study in school, and he is worried about his work schedule.

1. Problems are often called *obstacles*. Check (✓) Amad's obstacles.

- ☐ He doesn't speak English.
- ☐ He needs to get a full-time job.
- ☐ He is good with computers.
- ☐ He doesn't know what college to go to.
- ☐ He wants a degree.
- ☐ He doesn't know what to study in school.
- ☐ He doesn't have enough money for a family.
- ☐ He wants a better job.

2. What are some things he needs to do?

- ☐ He doesn't speak English.
- ☐ He needs to get a full-time job.
- ☐ He needs to study English.
- ☐ He needs to learn about colleges.
- ☐ He wants a degree.
- ☐ He needs to look for a full-time job.
- ☐ He wants a better job.
- ☐ He needs to talk to a counselor about what to study in school.

B. Look at the problems and solutions.

Hector's problems	Solutions				
	Asked a friend	Called the police	Went to school	Asked the teacher	Searched the Internet
He didn't speak English.			✗		
He didn't have a job.					✗
He needed to find a home for his family.	✗				
He had an emergency.		✗			

C. Use the information in Exercise B to write sentences.

1. *Hector went to school because he didn't speak English.*
2. ______________________________
3. ______________________________
4. ______________________________

D. Read the chart.

Simple Past with *So*							
Base	Affirmative	Negative		Base	Affirmative	Negative	
		didn't	base			*didn't*	base
ask	asked	didn't	ask	go	went	didn't	go
look	looked		look	have	had	didn't	have
talk	talked		talk	speak	spoke	didn't	speak
call	called		call	know	knew	didn't	know

Usage: a. and b. mean the same.

a. He talked to the teacher because he didn't speak English.

b. He didn't speak English, *so* he talked to the teacher.

a. He looked in the newspaper because he didn't have a job.

b. He didn't have a job, *so* he looked in the newspaper.

E. Look at the problems and solutions. Then, write three sentences with *because* and three sentences with *so*.

Tuba's problem	Solution		
	Looked in the phone book	Talked to a counselor	Asked the teacher
She didn't know where to find information about citizenship.		✗	
She didn't know how to read a bus schedule.			✗
She needed to find a school for her children.	✗		

because

1. Tuba talked to a counselor because she didn't know where to find information about citizenship.
2. She asked the teacher because ______
3. ______

so

1. ______
2. ______
3. ______

F. Rewrite the sentences in Exercise C with *so* instead of *because*.

1. Hector didn't speak English so he went to school.
2. ______
3. ______
4. ______

G. Write two of your problems and solutions. Then, write sentences.

Your problems	Solutions
1.	
2.	

UNIT 8

LESSON 5 My goals

GOAL ■ Record goals

A. **Look at the information below. Write what you *will do, what you plan to do, what you hope to do*, and *what you won't do*.**

1. learn English I will learn English.
2. get married ______
3. graduate from college ______
4. make a lot of money ______
5. be successful ______
6. have children ______
7. get a new job ______
8. help my family learn English ______
9. buy a home ______
10. send my children to a good school ______

B. **Write a paragraph using four or five of the sentences you wrote in Exercise A.**

C. Read the paragraph and complete the timeline.

My Goals

I have many goals for the next five years. Right now, I am studying at Lincoln Adult School. First, in 2016 and 2017 I'll learn English. I'll come to school every day. Next, in 2018 I hope to get a high school diploma and register at the local college. Then, in 2019 I plan to find a job. Finally, in 2020 I'll graduate with an AA degree and get a better job.

2016	2017	2018	2019	2020
I will learn English.				

D. Read the chart.

Transition Words in Sentences		
With numbers	Without numbers	Example sentence
First (First of all)	**First**	**First of all,** I went to town. / **First,** I went to town.
Second	**Next**	**Second,** I ate. / **Next,** I ate.
Third	**Then**	**Third,** I saw a movie. / **Then,** I saw a movie.
	After that	**After that,** I had a soda.
Finally / Lastly	**Finally**	**Lastly,** I went home. / **Finally,** I went home.
• Do not use numbers as transition words if there are more than four steps. • When not using numbers, *next*, *then*, and *after that* can be used in any order to describe more than one step. • Always finish with the words *finally* or *lastly*.		

E. **Read Gabriel's timeline again and write a paragraph about his future goals. Use transition words.**

2016	2018	2020	2022	2024	2026
work in my father's restaurant go to cooking school	cook new foods in my father's restaurant save money	buy a restaurant and serve international food	find a business partner start a second restaurant	find another business partner start another restaurant	hire managers for all restaurants

Gabriel will work in his father's restaurant.

F. **Look again at your timeline on page 132 and write a paragraph. Use transition words that are not numbers.**

PRACTICE TEST

A. Read and circle the correct answers.

Alena is a student at Ridge Adult School. She wants to get a high school diploma, but first she needs to start learning English. Her goal is to study English from 2016 to 2018. In 2018, she will take adult secondary education classes like history, science, and math. Next, she will to start college. She wants an AA degree and to start a nursing program. Alena is a good student. She hopes to work in the nursing field by 2022. Of course, obstacles can make it difficult. She needs to continue to work at her job at night and go to school during the day.

1. When does Alena want to start working as a nurse?
   a. 2016 b. 2018
   c. 2020 d. 2022
2. What does she want to complete in college?
   a. high school diploma b. AA degree
   c. nursing certificate d. GED
3. When does Alena work?
   a. at night b. She doesn't work.
   c. in the mornings d. part-time
4. What is Alena's first goal?
   a. be a nurse b. get an AA degree
   c. get a high school diploma d. learn English
5. What is Alena's final goal?
   a. be a nurse b. get an AA degree
   c. get a high school diploma d. learn English
6. Right now, Alena…
   a. speaks English a little. b. doesn't speak English.
   c. speaks English well. d. doesn't want to speak English.

GLOSSARY OF GRAMMAR TERMS

adjective	a word that describes a noun (Example: the *red* hat)
adverb	a word that modifies a verb, adjective, or another adverb (Example: She eats *quickly*.)
affirmative	not negative and not a question (Example: *I like him*.)
apostrophe	a punctuation mark that shows missing letters in contractions or possession (Example: *It's* or *Jim's*)
article	words used before a noun (Example: *a, an, the*)
base form	the main form of a verb, used without *to* (Example: *be, have, study*)
comma	a punctuation mark used to indicate a pause or separation (Example: I live in an apartment, and you live in a house.)
complement	a word or words that add to or complete an idea after the verb (Example: He is *happy*.)
conjugation	the form of a verb (Example: I *am*, You *are*, We *are*, They *are*, He *is*, She *is*, It *is*)
continuous form	a verb form that expresses action during time (Example: He *is shopping*.)
contraction	shortening of a word, syllable, or word group by omission of a sound or letter (Example: It is = *It's*, does not = *doesn't*)
count nouns	nouns that can be counted by number (Example: one *apple*, two *apples*)
definite article	use of *the* when a noun is known to speaker and listener (Example: I know *the* store.)
exclamation mark	a punctuation symbol marking surprise or emotion (Example: Hello!)
formal	polite or respectful language (Example: *Could* you *please* give me that?)
imperative	a command form of a verb (Example: *Listen*! or *Look out*!)
indefinite article	*a* or *an* used before a noun when something is talked about for the first time or when *the* is too specific (Example: There's *a* new restaurant.)
infinitive	the main form of a verb, usually used with *to* (Example: I like *to run* fast.)
informal	friendly or casual language (Example: *Can* I have that?)
irregular verb	a verb different from regular form verbs (Example: be = *am, are, is, was, were, being*)
modal auxiliary	a verb that indicates a mood (ability, possibility, etc.) and is followed by the base form of another verb (Example: I *can read* English well.)
modifier	a word phrase that describes another (Example: a *good* friend)
negative	the opposite of affirmative (Example: She *does not like* meat.)
noun	a name of a person, place, or thing (Example: *Joe, England, bottle*)
noncount nouns	nouns impossible or difficult to count (Example: *water, love, rice, fire*)

object, direct	the focus of a verb's action (Example: I eat *oranges*.)
object pronoun	replaces the noun taking the action (Example: *Julia* is nice. I like *her*.)
past tense	a verb form used to express an action or state in the past (Example: You *worked* yesterday.)
period	a punctuation mark ending a sentence (.)
plural	indicating more than one (Example: *pencils*, *children*)
possessive adjective	an adjective expressing possession (Example: *our* car)
preposition	a word that indicates relationship between objects (Example: *on* the *desk*)
present tense	a verb tense representing the current time, not past or future (Example: They *are* at home right now.)
pronoun	a word used in place of a noun (Example: *Ted* is 65. *He* is retired.)
question form	to ask or look for an answer (Example: *Where is my book?*)
regular verb	verb with endings that are regular and follow the rule (Example: work = *work*, *works*, *worked*, *working*)
sentence	a thought expressed in words, with a subject and verb (Example: *Julia works hard*.)
short answer	a response to a *yes/no* question, usually a subject pronoun and auxiliary verb (Example: *Yes, I am*, or *No, he doesn't*.)
singular	one object (Example: *a cat*)
statement	a sentence or thought (Example: *The weather is rainy today*.)
subject	the noun that does the action in a sentence (Example: *The gardener* *works* here.)
subject pronoun	a pronoun that takes the place of a subject (Example: *John* is a sudent. *He* is smart.)
syllable	a part of a word as determined by vowel sounds and rhythm (Example: *ta*-*ble*)
tag questions	short informal questions that come at the end of sentences in speech (Example: You like soup, *don't you?* They aren't hungry, *are they?*)
tense	the part of a verb that shows the past, present, or future time (Example: He *talked*.)
verb	word describing an action or state (Example: The boys *walk* to school. I *am* tired.)
vowels	the letters *a, e, i o, u,* and sometimes *y*
***wh-* questions**	questions that ask for information, usually starting with *Who, What, When, Where,* or *Why*. (Example: *Where* do you live?) *How* is often included in this group.
***yes/no* questions**	questions that ask for an affirmative or a negative answer (Example: *Are you happy?*)

GRAMMAR REFERENCE

Simple Present: *Be*			
Subject	**Verb**	**Residence**	**Example sentence**
I	am	from Mexico	**I am** from Mexico. *(I'm)*
We, You, They	are	single 23 years old	We **are** single. *(We're)* You **are** 23 years old. *(You're)*
He, She	is	divorced from Vietnam	He **is** divorced. *(He's)* She **is** from Vietnam. *(She's)*

Negative Statements with *Be*				
Subject	**Negative *be***	**Information**	**Contracted forms**	
I	**am not**	nervous.	**I'm not**	—
You	**are not**	in Houston.	you**'re not**	you **aren't**
He, She, It	**is not**	short.	he**'s**, she**'s**, it**'s** not	he, she, it **isn't**
We	**are not**	hungry.	we**'re not**	we **aren't**
They	**are not**	from Korea.	they**'re not**	they **aren't**

- There is only one contracted form for *I am not: I'm not.*
- There are two contracted forms for the other negative forms of *be*.

Yes/No Questions with *Be*				
Be	**Subject**	**Information**	**Example question**	**Short answer**
am	I	happy	**Am** I happy?	Yes, I am. / No, I'm not.
are	you	married	**Are** you married?	Yes, you are. / No, you're not.
	we	friends	**Are** we friends?	Yes, we are. / No, we're not.
	they	brothers	**Are** they brothers?	Yes, they are. / No, they're not.
is	he	from Italy	**Is** he from Italy?	Yes, he is. / No, he's not.
	she	in class today	**Is** she in class today?	Yes, she is. / No, she's not.
	it	sunny today	**Is** it sunny today?	Yes, it is. / No, it's not.

Questions with *Be*		
Question word	***Be***	**Singular or Plural**
Where	is	the milk? the water? the oil?
Where	**are**	the eggs? the bananas? the pears?

Answers with *Be*		
Subject	***Be***	**Location**
The milk It	**is**	in Aisle 1.
The eggs They	**are**	in Aisle 5.

Simple Present			
Subject	**Verb**	**Information**	**Example sentence**
I, You, We, They	eat go help play	lunch to school with the children soccer	I always **eat** lunch at 4:00 p.m. You often **go** to school at 8:00 a.m. We sometimes **help** with the children. They never **play** soccer on Saturday.
He, She	eats goes helps plays	lunch to school with the children soccer	He rarely **eats** lunch at 12:00 p.m. Nadia always **goes** to school early. Gilberto never **helps** with the children. She sometimes **plays** soccer on Friday.

Affirmative Simple Present		
I You We They	**wear** **like** **want** **need**	shoes
He She	**wears** **likes** **wants** **needs**	

Negative Simple Present			
I You We They	**do not** **(don't)**	**wear** **like** **want** **need**	sandals
He She	**does not** **(doesn't)**		

Simple Present: *Yes/No* Questions				
***Yes/No* question**			**Short answer**	
Do	I you we they	**need** a coat?	Yes, you **do**. Yes, I **do**. Yes, we **do**. Yes, they **do**.	No, you **don't**. No, I **don't**. No, we **don't**. No, they **don't**.
Does	he she it	**wear** sweaters?	Yes, he **does**. Yes, she **does**. Yes, it **does**.	No, he **doesn't**. No, she **doesn't**. No, it **doesn't**.

- Use *do* with *I, you, we, they*, and plural subjects.
- Use *does* with *he, she, it*, and singular subjects.
- Always use the base form after *do* or *does*.

Simple Present: *Live*			
Subject	**Verb**	**Residence**	**Example sentence**
I, We, You, They	live	in Los Angeles in California	I **live** in Los Angeles. You **live** in Los Angeles, California.
He, She	lives	in the United States in Mexico	He **lives** in the United States. She **lives** in Mexico.

Simple Present: *Have*			
Subject	***Have***	**Information**	**Example sentence**
I, You, We, They	have	three brothers two sisters	I **have** three brothers. We **have** two sisters.
He, She	has	no cousins three sons	He **has** no cousins. She **has** three sons.

Negative: *Have*				
Subject	**Negative**	***Have***	**Information**	**Example Sentence**
I, You, We, They	don't	have	three brothers two sisters	I **don't have** three brothers. We **don't have** three sisters.
He, She	doesn't		cousins three sons	He **doesn't have** cousins. She **doesn't have** three sons.

Yes/No Questions: *Is it?*				
Question + verb	**Information**	**Question**	**Answer**	
			Yes	***No***
Is it	hot windy cloudy rainy snowy cold foggy	**Is it** hot outside? **Is it** windy today? **Is it** cloudy in Florida? **Is it** rainy there? **Is it** snowy in the mountains? **Is it** cold in Chicago? **Is it** foggy in the morning?	Yes, **it is.**	No, **it isn't.**

Information Questions with *Be* and *Do*			
Information word	***Be***	**Information**	**Example answer**
How much (money)	**is** **are**	the rent? the flowers?	$1,500 a month. $20.00.
Where	**is** **are**	the apartment? the apartments?	On First Street.
What kind of home **What kinds** of homes	**is** **are**	for rent? in the neighborhood?	An apartment. Apartments and houses.
Information word	***Do* + subject**	**Base verb**	**Example answer**
How much (money)	**do** you	**have?**	$20.00.
Where	**do** you	**live?**	On First Street.
What kind of home **What kinds** of homes	**do** you **do** you	**have?**	An apartment. Apartments and houses.
How many bedrooms	**does** it	**have?**	Three.

Information Question	Example answer
What is your name?	My name is Javier Aguilar.
Where do you live now?	I live in Santa Clara.
Where did you live before?	I lived in Richmond.
How long did you live there?	I lived there three years.
Who is your employer?	I work for Anchor Motors.
What is your position?	I am a mechanic.

Information Questions with *which*				
Information word	**Subject**	**Verb**	**Information**	**Example question**
Which	house	has	three bedrooms a pool a fireplace a big yard	**Which** house has three bedrooms?
	houses	have		**Which** houses have three bedrooms?
	house	is	on First Street next to the park	**Which** house is on First Street?
	houses	are		**Which** houses are on First Street? **Which** houses are next to the park?

Present Continuous			
Subject	*Be*	Base+*ing*	Example sentence
I	am	writing	**I am writing** this letter in English.
You, We, They	are	going	We **are going** to the mall.
He, She	is	eating	He **is eating** at the coffee shop.

- Use simple present with *always, often, usually, never, sometimes,* and *every day.*
- Use the present continuous with *right now, at this moment,* and *today.*

Affirmative Present Continuous			
Subject	*Be*	Base + *ing*	
I	**am**	**wearing** **buying** **going** **shopping** **eating**	right now
You, We, They	**are**		at this moment
He, She, It	**is**		today

Negative Present Continuous				
Subject	*Be*	*not*	Base + *ing*	
I (I'm)	**am**	**not**	**waiting** **buying** **going** **shopping** **eating**	right now
You, We, They	**are**	**not (aren't)**		at this moment
He, She, It	**is**	**not (isn't)**		today

Present Continuous: *Yes/No* Questions				
Be	Subject	Base verb + *ing*	Short answer	
Am	I	**going** with you to the mall?	Yes, you **are**.	No, you **aren't**.
Are	you	**shopping** today?	Yes, I **am**.	No, **I'm not**.
Is	he, she, it	**wearing** a sweater?	Yes, he/she/it **is**.	No, he/she/it **isn't**.
Are	we	**buying** new jeans now?	Yes, we **are**.	No, we **aren't**.
Are	they	**having** a sale right now?	Yes, they **are**.	No, they **aren't**.

Regular Simple Past	
Subject	Verb (base + *ed*)
I, You, He, She, We, They	**walked (walk)** **talked (talk)** **smoked (smoke)** **played (play)**

Irregular Simple Past	
Subject	Verb
I, You, He, She, We, They	**had (have)** **went (go)** **said (say)**

Irregular Simple Past: *Be*		
Subject	*Be*	Example sentence
I, He, She	**was**	I **was** sick.
You, We, They	**were**	You **were** at the hospital.

Simple Past (Regular)		
Subject	Verb (base+*ed*)	Example sentence
I, You, He, She, It, We, They	talked wanted walked	I **talked** with Marie. She **wanted** a sandwich. We **walked** in the park.

Simple Past (Irregular)		
Subject	Verb	Example sentence
I, You, He, She, It, We, They	went (go) ate (eat) bought (buy) sent (send)	I **went** to the park. She **ate** at the coffee shop. We **bought** new dresses. They **sent** a letter.

Simple Past: Questions		
Yes/No Question	Short answer	
Did you **exercise** yesterday?	Yes, I **did**.	No, I **didn't**.
Did he **have** an earache?	Yes, he **did**.	No, he **didn't**.
Did we **buy** any aspirin?	Yes, we **did**.	No, we **didn't**.
• For *yes/no* questions in the simple past tense (regular or irregular verbs), use *did* + the base form.		
Information Question	Answer	
Where **did** you **play** soccer yesterday?	I played soccer in the park.	
How **did** she **get** to the doctor's office?	She took the bus.	
When **did** they **have** an appointment?	They had an appointment at 3:00.	
• For information questions in the simple past tense, use *did* + the base form.		

Simple Past	
Negative forms of regular and irregular verbs (except *be*)	
I **didn't work** in the evenings.	We **didn't have** a paid vacation.
Dalva **didn't know** how to type.	You **didn't turn off** the computer.
• For all forms of regular and irregular verbs (except *be*), use *did not* (*didn't*) + base.	
Negative forms of *be*	
I **wasn't** at work today. He/She/It **wasn't** friendly.	We **weren't** happy. You **weren't** in the hospital. They **weren't** at the front desk.
• For the verb *be*, use *was not* (*wasn't*) and *were not* (*weren't*).	

Questions with *Can*			
Can	**Subject**	**Base verb**	**Example sentence**
can	I	take help	**Can** I take your order? **Can** I help you?
can	you		**Can** you take my order? **Can** you take our order, please? **Can** you help me? **Can** you help us?

Questions with *May* and *Can*			
Can	**Subject**	**Base verb**	**Example question and answer**
can	I, you, he, she, it, we, they	type drive understand work cook clean talk	**Can** you type letters? Yes, I can. **Can** they drive a car? No, they can't. **Can** she understand English? Yes, she can. **Can** I work on Saturdays? Yes, you can. **Can** he cook breakfast? No, he can't. **Can** we clean on the weekend? Yes, you can. **Can** you talk to customers? No, you can't.

Modal: *Can* (Ability)				
	Subject	***Can***	**Base verb**	**Example sentence**
Affirmative	I	**can**	type	I **can** type 60 words a minute.
	he, she, it	**can**	use	He/ She **can** use a computer.
	we	**can**	fix	We **can** fix things around the house.
Negative	you	**cannot**	speak	You **cannot** speak Spanish.
	they	**can't**	turn	They **can't** turn on the copier.
• The negative of *can* is *cannot*. The contraction is *can't*.				

Modals: *May* and *Might* to Show Probability (Use Interchangeably)			
Subject	Modal	Base verb	Example sentence
I, You, He, She, It, We, They	may might	spend earn be	I **may** spend $250 on gasoline this month. You **may** spend $175 on the phone bill. He **may** earn $6,000. Food **might** be $1,000. We **may** earn $3,500 a month. They **may** spend $300 a month on food.

Questions with *Should*	
Yes/No Question	Short answer
Should I **exercise** every day?	Yes, you **should**. No, you **shouldn't**.
Should he **have** a checkup?	Yes, he **should**. No, he **shouldn't**.
Should we **buy** some vitamins?	Yes, we **should**. No, we **shouldn't**.
Information Question	Answer
Who **should** I **ask** about the medicine?	You **should** ask the doctor.
Where **should** she **buy** the cough syrup?	She **should** buy the cough syrup at the pharmacy.
Why **should** we **take** the pills?	We have a cough and a fever.
• For *Yes/No* questions and information questions, use *should* + the base form.	

Modal: *Should*			
Subject	*Should*	Base verb	Example sentence
I, You, He, She, We, They	should	take talk take swallow	I **should** take two tablets. He **should** talk to the doctor. You **should** take this medicine for a headache. They **should** swallow this tablet with water.

Modal: *Shouldn't*			
Subject	*Should*	Base verb	Example sentence
I, You, He, She, We, They	should not shouldn't	take chew drink	You **shouldn't** take this pill with other medicine. He **shouldn't** drink alcohol with this medicine. She **shouldn't** chew this tablet.

Future: *Will*			
Subject	*Will*	Base verb	Information
I, You, He, She, It, We, They	will	go	to school for two more years
		study	English this year
		be	a nurse
want to *hope to* *plan to* *be going to* *will* less definite ————————→ very definite			

Future: *Will* (Affirmative)			
Subject	***Will***	**Base verb**	**Example sentence**
I, You, He, She, We, They	will	come listen help work have	I **will** come to class on time. You **will** listen carefully and follow instructions. They **will** help other students. We **will** work hard. He **will** have a positive attitude.

Future: *Will* (Negative)			
Subject	***Will***	**Base verb**	**Example sentence**
I, You, He, She, We, They	will not (won't)	come leave forget	I **won't** come to class late. I **won't** leave class early. I **won't** forget my homework.

Yes/No Questions with *Will*			
Statement	**Question**	**Answer**	
I will be rich some day.	**Will** I **be** rich some day?	Yes, you will.	No, you won't.
You will start college next year.	**Will** you **start** college next year?	Yes, I will.	No, I won't.
He will find a job.	**Will** he **find** a job?	Yes, he will.	No, he won't.
She will get some advice.	**Will** she **get** some advice?	Yes, she will.	No, she won't.
It will be closed.	**Will** it **be** closed?	Yes, it will.	No, it won't.
We will work together.	**Will** we **work** together?	Yes, we will.	No, we won't.
They will handle the money.	**Will** they **handle** the money?	Yes, they will.	No, they won't.

Express Future Plans: *want to, hope to, plan to*			
Subject	**Verb**	**Infinitive (*to* + base)**	
I, You, We, They	**hope, want, plan**	to	**study** in school for three years **graduate** from college **get** married **be** a doctor
He, She	**hopes, wants, plans**		

Express Future Plans: *Be going to*			
Subject	***Be going to***	**Base verb**	**Information**
I	**am going to**	get	a high school diploma
You, We, They	**are going to**	participate	in my child's school
He, She	**is going to**	buy	a house

Will/Be going to: Information Questions	
Wh- word + *will* + subject + base verb	*Wh-* word + *be* + subject + *going to* + base verb
What **will** you do tomorrow?	What **are** you **going to** do tomorrow?
What time **will** she leave?	What time **is** she **going to** leave?
How **will** you pay for school?	How **are** you **going to** pay for school?
When **will** they arrive?	When **are** they **going to** arrive?
How much time **will** the students have?	How much time **are** the students **going to** have?
How long **will** they stay?	How long **are** they **going to** stay?
How often **will** you take a trip?	How often **are** you **going to** take a trip?
Where **will** she live?	Where **is** she **going to** live?

Using *Because*			
		Reason	
Statement	*Because*	Subject + verb	Example sentence
I want the blue shirt	because	it is cheaper	I want the blue shirt **because** it is cheaper.
I shop at Addy's	because	it is close	I shop at Addy's **because** it is close to my home.
You like the shirt	because	it is green	You like the shirt **because** it is green.

Because and Adverbial Clauses			
		Reason	
Statement		Subject + verb	Information
Maria plans to go to college	**because**	she wants	to be a nurse
Lien hopes to learn English better		she plans	to go to college

Examples: Maria plans to go to college **because** she wants to be a nurse.
Lien hopes to learn English **because** she plans to go to college.

Usage:
- Usually you do not write a comma after or before *because*.
- A subject always follows *because*.

Combining Sentences with *and*			
Subject		Subject	
The house	<u>is</u> in a quiet neighborhood.	**The house**	<u>has</u> a swimming pool.
The house	<u>is</u> in a quiet neighborhood, **and**	**it**	<u>has</u> a swimming pool.
The house is in a quiet neighborhood, **and it** has a swimming pool.			

Combining Sentences with *and*			
Subject		Subject	
The rooms	<u>have</u> air-conditioning.	**The rooms**	<u>are</u> in good condition.
The rooms	<u>have</u> air-conditioning, **and**	**they**	<u>are</u> in good condition.
The rooms have air-conditioning, **and they** are in good condition.			

Verb + Infinitive			
Subject	Verb	Infinitive (*to* + base)	Example sentence
I, You, We, They	want	to sleep	I **want to sleep** eight hours.
	need	to relax	You **need to relax** after work.
	like	to work	We **like to work** in the morning.
He, She	wants	to drink	They **want to drink** a lot of water.
	needs	to eat	He **likes to eat** a snack in the afternoon.
	likes	to exercise	She **likes to exercise** regularly.

Imperatives	
Affirmative imperative	Negative imperative
Write your name on the application.	**Don't write** your age.
Press the green button.	**Don't press** the red button.
Be helpful at work.	**Don't be** late for work.

- The imperative uses the base form of the verb.
- The subject is **you**, but it is not included.
- The negative imperative is *do not* + base form. The contraction is *don't*.
- Imperatives give warnings, directions, or suggestions.
- Use an exclamation mark (!) if the feeling is very strong.

Adjective	Comparative adjective	Example sentence
cheap	**cheaper**	The shirt is **cheaper** *than* the dress.
expensive	**more expensive**	The shoes are **more expensive** *than* the shirt.
	less expensive	The dress is **less expensive** *than* the jacket.
Adjective	**Superlatives**	**Example sentence**
cheap	**cheapest**	The socks are the **cheapest**.
expensive	**most expensive**	The jacket is the **most expensive**.
	least expensive	The socks are the **least expensive**.

Adjectives and noun modifiers	
Adjectives	**Noun modifiers**
Adjectives describe nouns. I live in a **friendly** neighborhood.	A noun can sometimes describe another noun. I need a **coffee** table.
Adjectives come before nouns. He likes the **big** yard.	The second noun is more general than the first. A **coffee** table is usually small.
Adjectives do not change for plural nouns. You're buying some **new** tables.	The first noun is always singular. Where are the **coffee** tables?
You can put two adjectives before a noun. Use a comma between the adjectives. We want a **large, old** house.	You can put a number before a noun modifier. Use a hyphen between the number and the modifier. You want a **two-bedroom** apartment. (Meaning: two bedrooms, not two apartments)

Transition Words in Sentences		
With numbers	**Without numbers**	**Example sentence**
First (First of all)	**First**	**First of all**, I went to town. **First**, I went to town.
Second	**Next**	**Second**, I ate. / **Next**, I ate.
Third	**Then**	**Third**, I saw a movie. / **Then**, I saw a movie.
	After that	**After that**, I had a soda.
Finally / Lastly	**Finally**	**Lastly**, I went home. / **Finally**, I went home.

- Do not use numbers as transition words if there are more than four steps.
- When not using numbers, *next, then,* and *after that* can be used in any order to describe more than one step.
- Always finish with the words *finally* or *lastly*.

Possessive Adjectives		
Pronoun	Possessive adjective	Example sentence
I	**my**	**My** address is 3356 Archer Blvd.
You	**your**	**Your** phone number is 555-5678.
He	**his**	**His** last name is Jones.
She	**her**	**Her** first name is Lien.
It	**its**	**Its** name is Crystal River Dam.
We	**our**	**Our** teacher is Mr. Kelley.
They	**their**	**Their** home is in Sausalito.

Demonstrative Adjectives: *this, that, these, those*		
	Near	Far
Singular	**this** sweater **this** hat	**that** sweater **that** hat
Plural	**these** shoes **these** pants	**those** shoes **those** pants

Example sentences		
	Near	Far
Singular	**This** sweater is perfect. I want **this** hat.	**That** sweater is blue. I like **that** hat.
Plural	**These** pants fit. I like **these** shoes.	**Those** pants are great! I like **those** shoes.

How much / How many	
Count nouns	Noncount nouns

Use *many* with nouns you can count.	Use *much* with nouns you cannot count.
Example Questions	
How many tomatoes do we need? **How many** pounds of tomatoes do we need?	**How much** flour do we need? **How much** rice do we need?

There is / There are	
Singular	**There is (There's)** a good Vietnamese restaurant in Portland. **There is (There's)** one bottle of soda for lunch.
Plural	**There are** carrots in Aisle 4. **There are** three pieces of cake.
Questions	**Is there** a dairy section in this supermarket? **Are there** many Chinese restaurants in Los Angeles?
• Use *there* to show or ask about place or position.	

Some / Any		
	Count (Plural)	Noncount
Affirmative	I eat **some** vegetables every day.	I often eat **some** rice for dinner.
Negative	I don't eat **any** cookies.	I don't eat **any** rice.
Question	Do you have **any** cookies? Do you want **some** cookies?	Do you have **any** rice? Do you want **some** rice?
• In questions that are requests or offers, use *some*.		

Prepositions of Location	
Preposition	Example
in	There is a hospital **in** Thomasville.
on	It is **on** Main Street.
at	It is **at** the intersection of Main Street and Northern Avenue.
near	It is **near** my house.
between	My house is **between** South Street and Washington Street.
next to	It is **next to** the police station.
on the corner (of)	The police station is **on the corner of** South Street and Pine Street.
across from	It is **across from** the post office.
on the right	The courthouse is **on the right**.
on the left	The fire station is **on the left**.

Prepositions of Time		
Preposition	Information	Example sentence
on	days dates	I am going to the bank **on** Saturday. City Hall is not open **on** July 4.
at	a specific time night	I am going to the dentist **at** 3:00 p.m. We go to the library **at** night.
in	amount of time months seasons *the morning / afternoon / evening*	He's going to Japan **in** two hours. He always visits his sister **in** August. The weather is very warm **in** the summer. We go to the bowling alley **in** the afternoon.

PHOTO CREDITS

3 (bl) David Young-Wolff/PhotoEdit, (bl) Michael Newman/PhotoEdit, (br) Tony Freeman/PhotoEdit, (br) Michael Newman/PhotoEdit, **8** (c) David Young-Wolff/PhotoEdit, (b) Michael Newman/PhotoEdit, **28** Mel Yates/Digital Vision/Getty Images, **56** Nitr/Shutterstock.com, **60** (tl) Baoba Images/Riser/Getty Images, (tr) Tony Freeman/PhotoEdit, **69** (tl) Ad Oculos/Shutterstock.com, (tl) StudioSmart/Shutterstock.com, (tr) lynnette/Shutterstock.com, (tr) Room27/Shutterstock.com,(cl) Sandratsky Dmitriy/Shutterstock.com, (cl) donatas1205/Shutterstock.com, (cr) Zhukova Valentyna/Shutterstock.com, (cr) James Marvin Phelps/Shutterstock.com, **93** (tl) David Young-Wolff/PhotoEdit, (tc) Tony Freeman/PhotoEdit, (tr) Michael Newman/PhotoEdit.